BRITISH
ARMORED
FIGHTING VEHICLES

GEORGE BRADFORD

STACKPOLE
BOOKS

Copyright © 2008 by George Bradford

Published by
STACKPOLE BOOKS
5067 Ritter Road
Mechanicsburg, PA 17055
www.stackpolebooks.com

Cover design by Wendy A. Reynolds

Printed in the United States of America

FIRST EDITION

Library of Congress Cataloging-in-Publication Data

Bradford, George.
  British armored fighting vehicles / George Bradford.
      p. cm. — (World War II AFV plans)
  Includes bibliographical references.
  ISBN-13: 978-0-8117-3453-0
  ISBN-10: 0-8117-3453-6
  1. Armored vehicles, Military—Great Britain—Drawings. 2. Tanks
(Military science)—Great Britain—Drawings. I. Title.

  UG446.5.B6824 2008
  623.7'475094109044—dc22

                                                    2007036633

CONTENTS

INTRODUCTION

Volume Five in this series of books on scale drawings of armored fighting vehicles of World War II is devoted to British and Commonwealth military vehicles that took part in the war. Many of these vehicles were quite unique and are shown here roughly in chronological order of appearance on the scene. However, there was much overlap in vehicle production, and this makes it somewhat difficult to establish a sequence that is totally perfect.

The coverage here will range from the prewar developments that led up to 1939 and the vehicles that saw action in the early battles of World War II. There was always the problem of staying abreast of your opponent in both weapons and armor protection, and this aspect would flow back and forth for five long years during the war. Among the vehicles covered you will find some of the prototypes that never really saw action, plus some of the vehicles that were just too late to participate in the war, but show the direction that armor development was going by war's end. You will also find that we cover mainly armored fighting vehicles, but a few support vehicles that fought along side of them are thrown in.

The ultimate purpose of this series of books is to try to present a sequence of World War II military vehicle plan view scale drawings all in one place. Most of these drawings display 4-view plans, but with some of the smaller vehicles, we were able to show five or more views. However, no matter how well the plans are drawn, it is always necessary to have sufficient photo reference books as well. There are a number of "walk around" and close-up view series on the market to give the super-detailers all the finer detail they could ask for.

Over the years, scale drawings of various armored vehicles have appeared in magazines and books, but never all in one place where they would be easy for the researcher or modeler to access them. Many different scales have fought for the lime-light, but the more popular ones of late have boiled down to mainly 1:35, 1:48, and 1:72 in the armor modeling world. With this in mind, we have tried to keep the drawings as large as possible with a preponderance of 1:35 scale drawings, supported by 1:48 scale where appropriate, and also for vehicles that are simply too big to fit on these pages comfortably as 1:35 scale drawings. The 1:72 scale plans are mainly used to fill out a page here and there, and give the modeler some choice.

You will also find a chart at the beginning of this book for reducing or enlarging any of these drawings to other popular scales. The quality and accuracy of modern photocopying should make it possible for you to achieve whatever final scale you require. However, in some cases where enlargement is required, you may only be able to squeeze one view onto letter size paper and may have to utilize 11" x 17" paper where available.

These drawings have been created using vector-based drawing applications with line weights ranging from .25 point to 1 point, and thus should easily hold the finer detail when copying. The bulk of these drawings were done over a period of ten years and are currently among the most precise and accurate AFV drawings available. You will also notice a variance in the drawings as the art style changes slightly over the years but eventually supports shading in the majority of the later works.

SCALE CONVERSIONS

REDUCING

1:35 to 1:48 Scale = 73%

1:35 to 1:76 Scale = 46%

1:35 to 1:72 Scale = 49%

1:35 to 1:87 Scale = 41%

1:48 to 1:76 Scale = 63%

1:48 to 1:72 Scale = 66%

1:48 to 1:87 Scale = 55%

1:72 to 1:76 Scale = 95%

ENLARGING

1:35 to 1:32 Scale = 109%

1:35 to 1:16 Scale = 218%

1:48 to 1:35 Scale = 138%

1:48 to 1:32 Scale = 150%

1:48 to 1:16 Scale = 300%

1:72 to 1:35 Scale = 207%

1:72 to 1:48 Scale = 150%

1:72 to 1:16 Scale = 450%

Carden-Loyd Mk. VI

Machine Gun Carrier

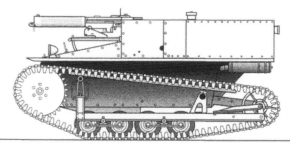

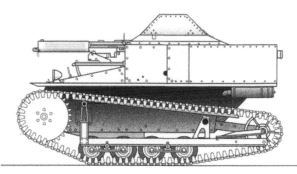

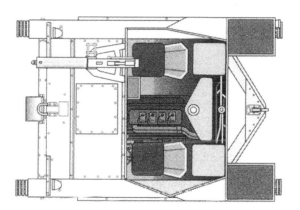

The basic Carden-Loyd Mk. VI with stowage boxes.

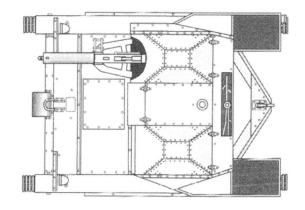

The Carden-Loyd Mk. VI with armored headcovers, supplied to Siam, USSR, Japan, Italy, South America and Asia.

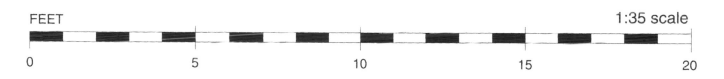

FEET

1:35 scale

0   5   10   15   20

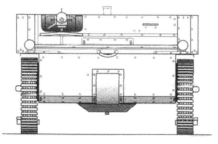

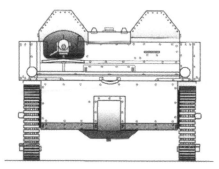

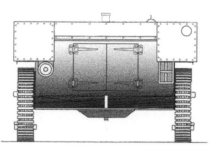

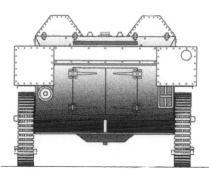

The Carden-Loyd was an extremely successful design, easy to build and simple to repair. It was a low-cost design that caught the eye of most of the major powers of the time. It spawned numerous look-alike imitations to equip armies around the world. Russia bought a few, copied the design, and produced the T-27; Italy built the CV-33; Poland, the TK-3; France, the Renault UE; and the Czechs took many of the salient features and came up with their MU-4.

However, when World War II broke out, it was soon realized that these vehicles were far too puny to survive on the new battlefields.

Rolls-Royce Armored Car
1924 Pattern, N. Africa 1940

The turret detail and interior is all provisional mainly because of the lack of good reference.

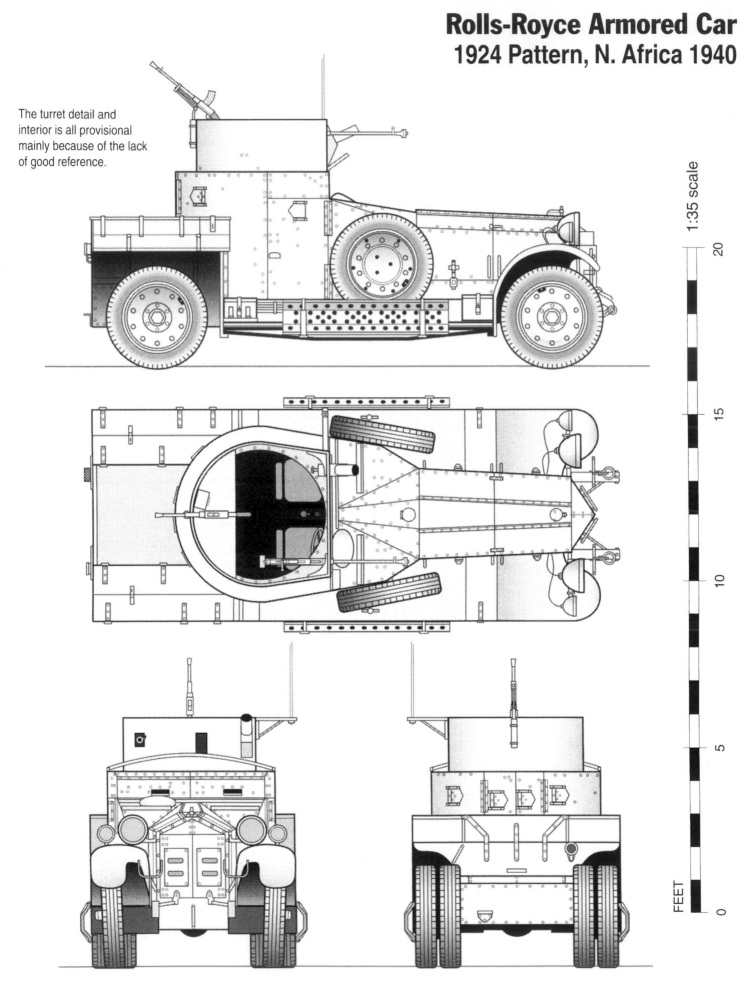

1:35 scale

FEET

Vickers Medium Mk. II Tank**

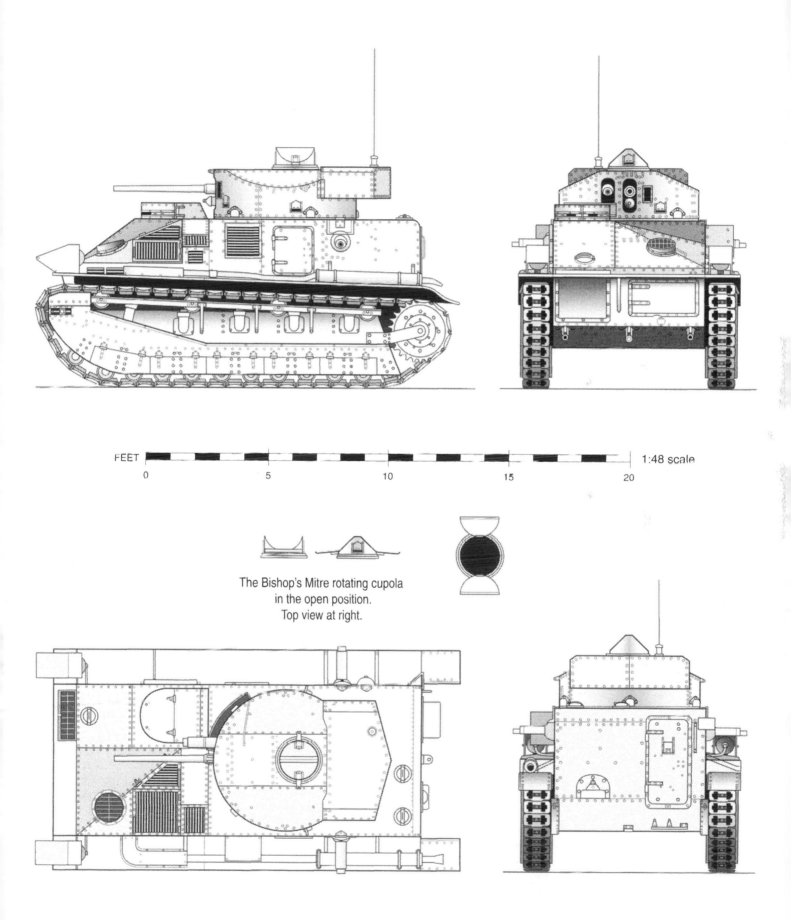

FEET

0   5   10   15   20

1:48 scale

The Bishop's Mitre rotating cupola
in the open position.
Top view at right.

Cruiser Tank, Mk. I (A9)

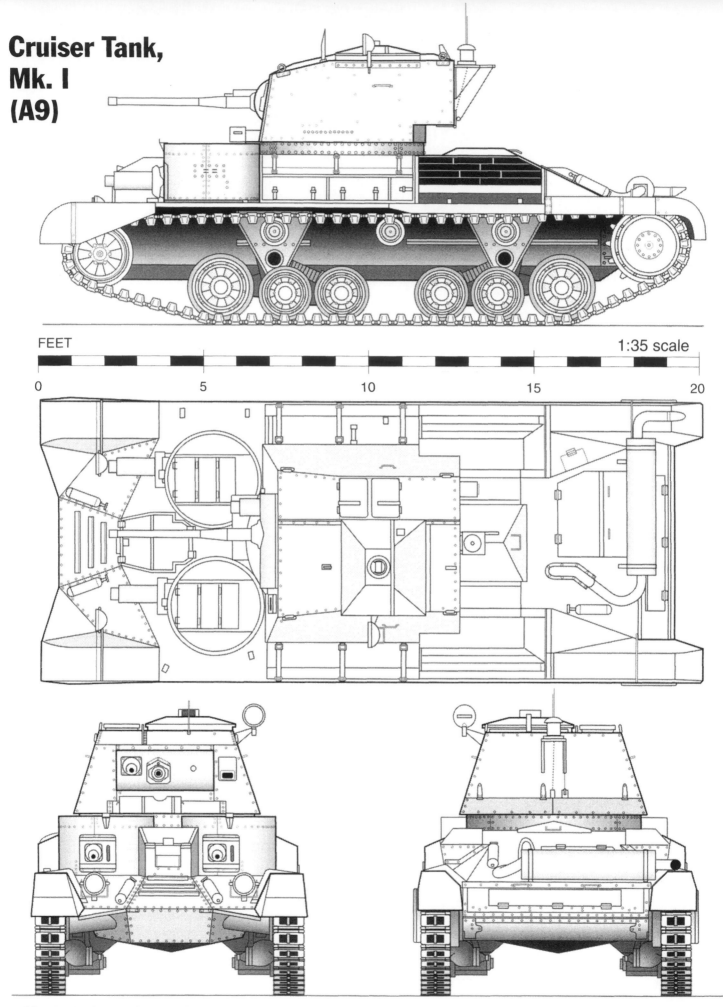

FEET

1:35 scale

0   5   10   15   20

Armored Car, Reconnaissance,
Morris Model CS9/LAC
11th Hussars, North Africa, 1940

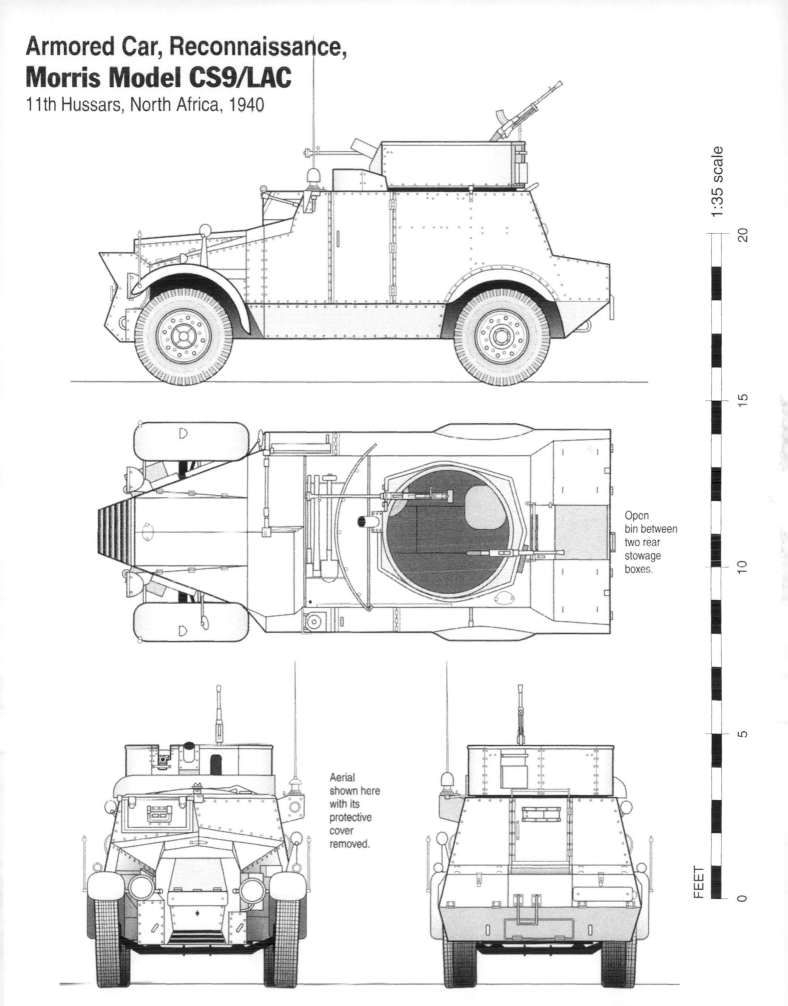

1:35 scale

Open bin between two rear stowage boxes.

Aerial shown here with its protective cover removed.

FEET

Infantry Tank, Mk. I (A11)
"Matilda I"

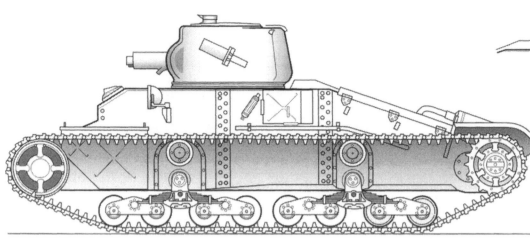

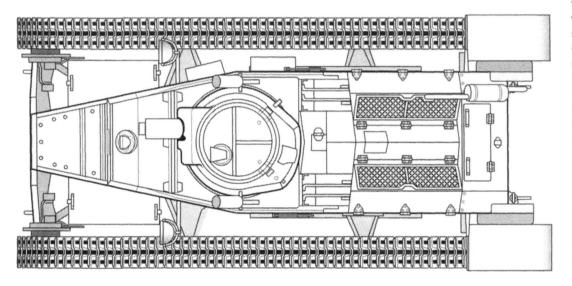

The "Tank, Infantry, Mark I" was specifically designed to accompany the infantry during an assault, and take anything the enemy could throw at it. Armed with only a machine gun, the crew of two had little interest in attacking other tanks.

The design was originated by Sir John Carden of the Vickers empire, and at the time the cost limitations of the 30s were still playing havoc with the defense industry. The strong point of the Infantry Tank Mk. I was the fact that it flaunted 60mm armor, which was invulnerable to any standard anti-tank guns the Germans had available at the outbreak of the war. When these British tanks were encountered at Arras, the only German gun that could stop them was the 88mm anti-aircraft gun forced into service as an anti-tank gun.

By 1937 they were in production and formed the greater part of the British 1st Army Tank Brigade in France, 1940, when the Germans attacked. The A11 gave a good account of itself, but its slow speed of 8mph and lack of a decent gun doomed it.

FEET

1:35 scale

0   5   10   15   20

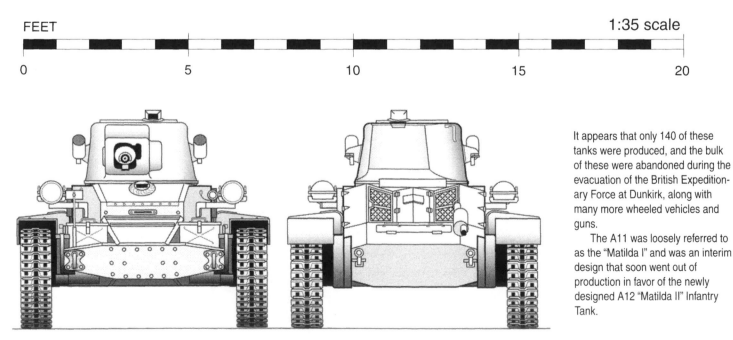

It appears that only 140 of these tanks were produced, and the bulk of these were abandoned during the evacuation of the British Expeditionary Force at Dunkirk, along with many more wheeled vehicles and guns.

The A11 was loosely referred to as the "Matilda I" and was an interim design that soon went out of production in favor of the newly designed A12 "Matilda II" Infantry Tank.

The early Cruiser Mark III, designated A13 Mk. I, already displaying some of the features that would carry the Walter J. Christie fast-track design over to British Cruiser tanks.

Cruiser Mark IVs, designated as A13 Mk. II, of the British 1st Armoured Division on maneuvers in England, 1939. It was soon to see action in France in 1940.

Cruiser Tank Mk. III
(A13 Mk. I)

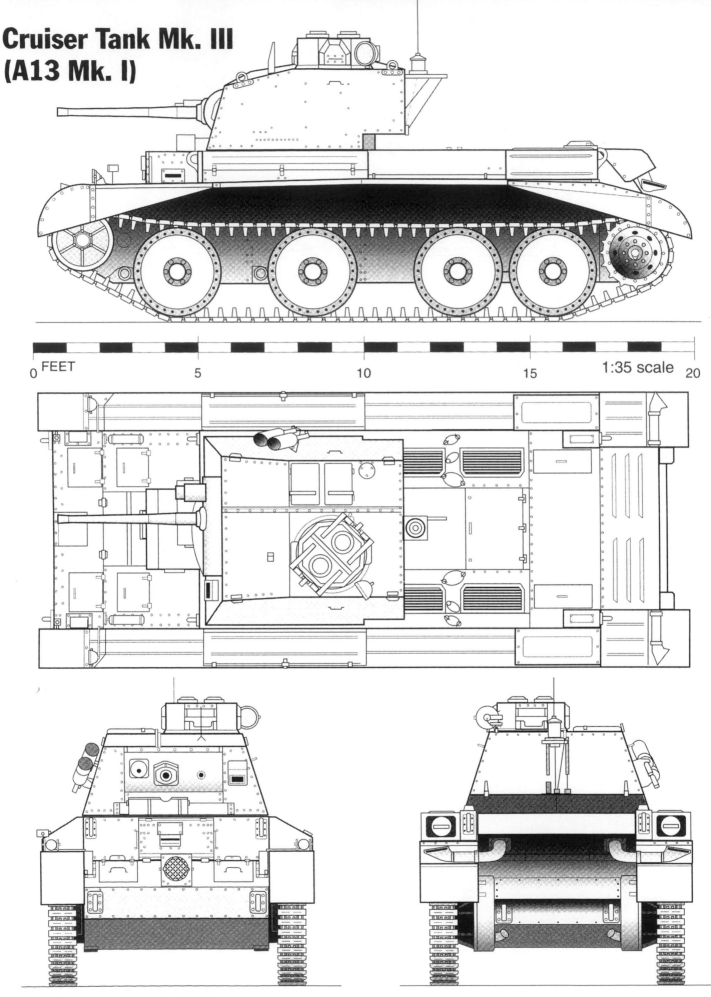

0 FEET　　　5　　　10　　　15　　　1:35 scale　20

Cruiser Tank Mk. IV (A13 Mk. II)

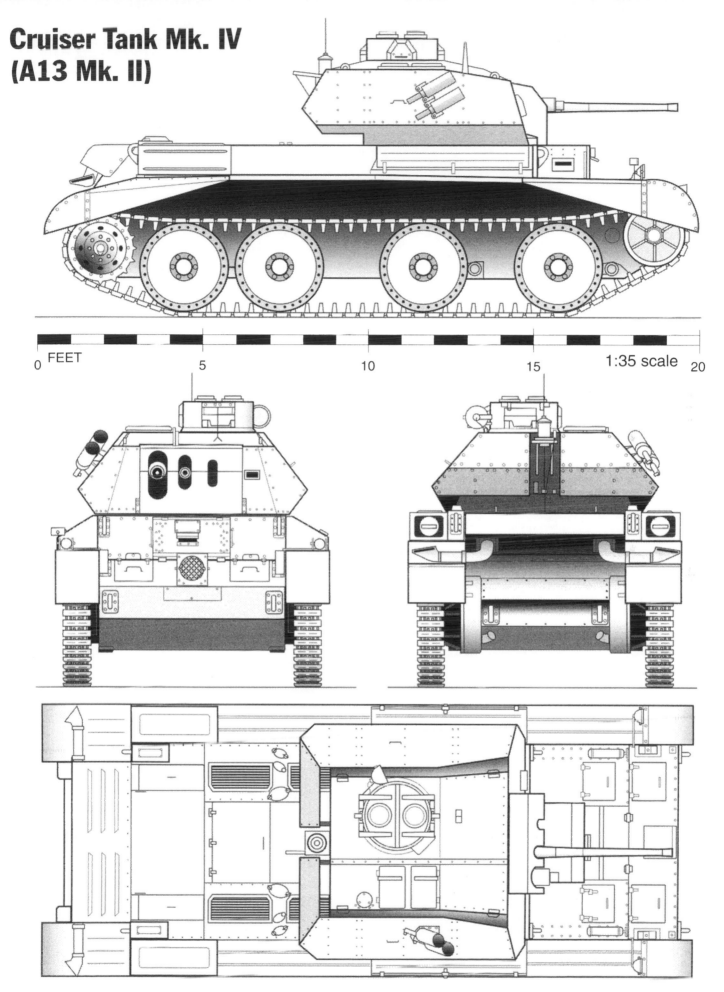

0 FEET   5   10   15   1:35 scale   20

Cruiser Tank Mk. IVA
(A13 Mk. II)
North Africa 1941

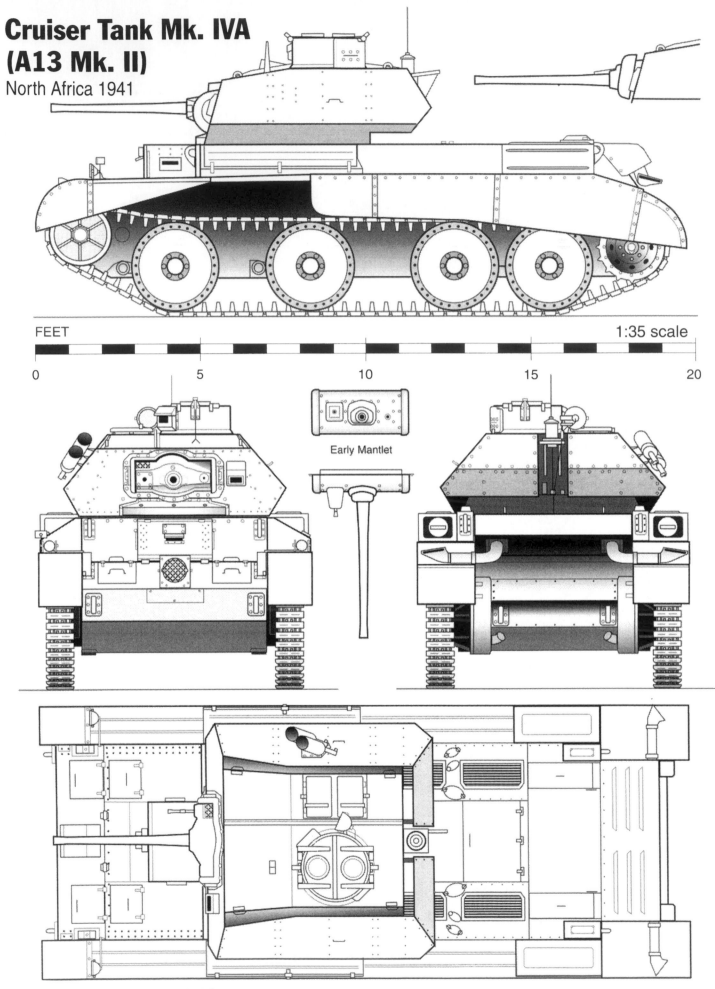

FEET

1:35 scale

0   5   10   15   20

Early Mantlet

Carrier, Universal
No. 1, Mk. I

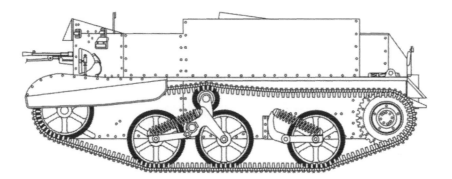

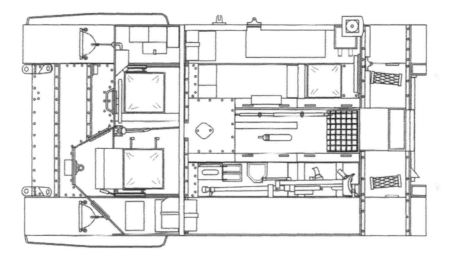

FEET

1:35 scale

0   5   10   15   20

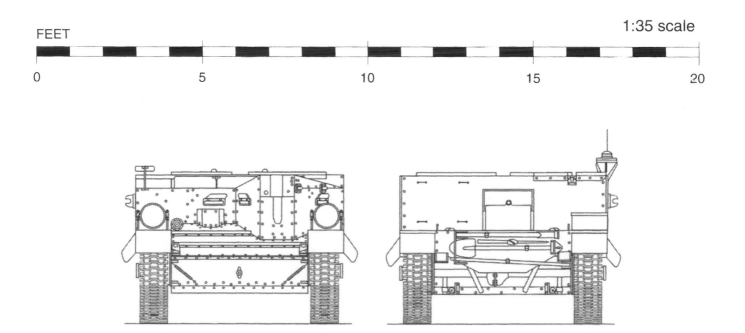

Loading a Universal Carrier onto an LVT "Buffalo" amphibious vehicle in the Po River area, Italy, circa 1943–44.

A close-up of the stowage in this rear view of a Bren Carrier No. 2, Mk. I.

Cruiser Tank, Mk. IIA (A10)

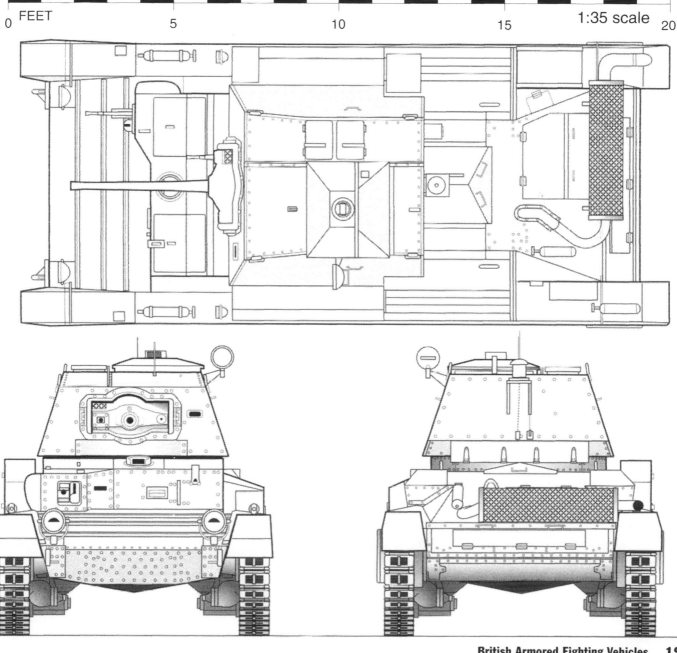

0 FEET   5   10   15   1:35 scale 20

Ford Indian Pattern Carrier Mk. IIA
(Armored Carrier, Wheeled, I.P. Mark IIA)

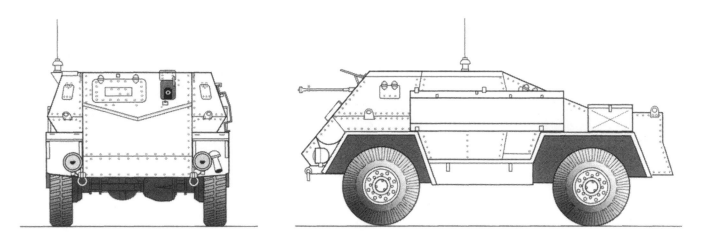

FEET

0   5   10   15   20

1:48 scale

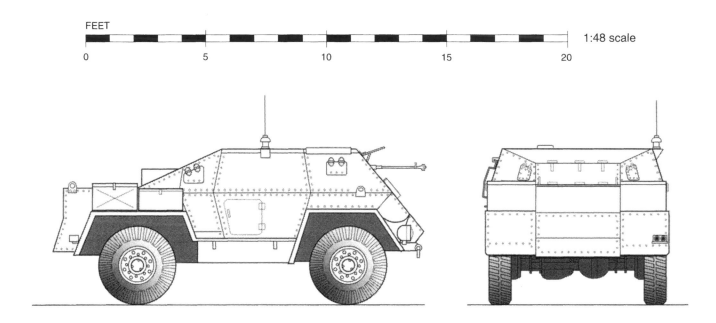

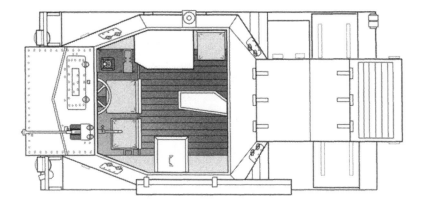

Infantry Tank, Mk. IIA (A12)
Matilda, Mk. II

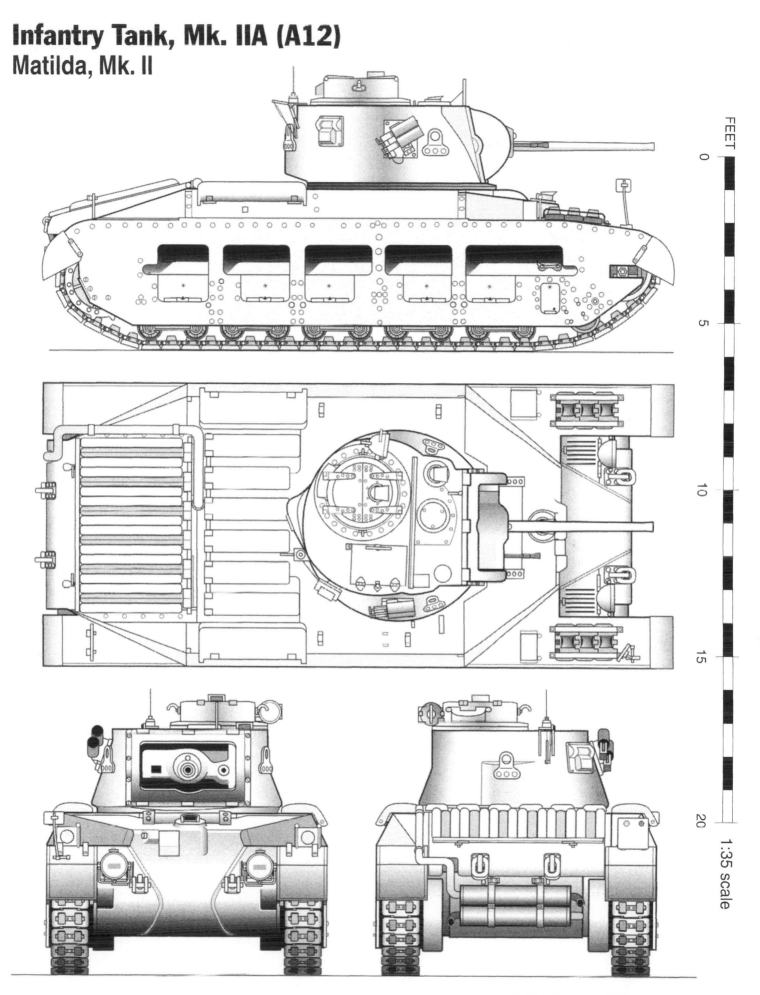

FEET

0

5

10

15

20

1:35 scale

A 27-ton Matilda II infantry tank moving up to Derna in the Western Desert, late January 1941.
The three-tone diagonal Caunter stripe pattern camouflage can still be seen at this time.

A full rear view of the Matilda infantry tank while on display as part of the Worthington Tank Museum at Canadian Forces Base at Borden, Ontario.

Light Tank Mk. VIA

North Africa, 1940

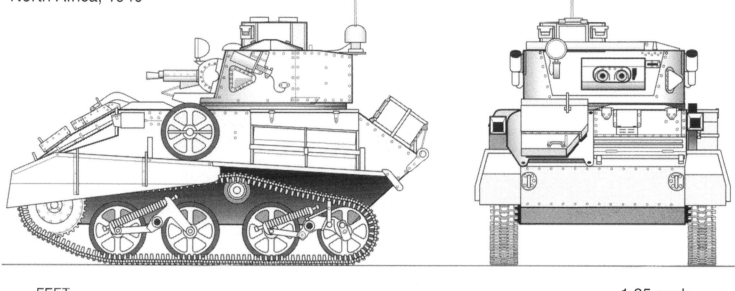

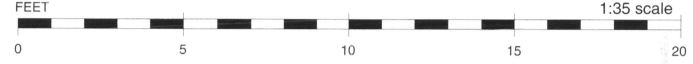

FEET

1:35 scale

0   5   10   15   20

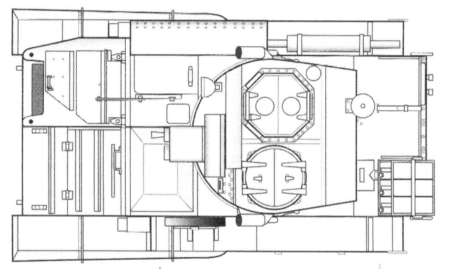

At the outbreak of World War II, the Light Tank Mk. VI was the most numerous tank in service with the British Army. They were used in France in 1940, where their shortcomings were soon recognized. However, after Dunkirk they were still the main tank on the homefront and abroad.

In 1938 the 1st (Light) Battalion returned to Egypt equipped with Mk. VIAs and VIBs, which eventually ended up fed into the early 7th Armoured Division in 1940. In June 1940 there were still 135 in use with 7th AD. These Vickers-Armstrong light tanks were intended for reconnaissance duties by then. However, because of the total lack of tanks in Egypt, they were forced into the "cruiser tank" role as well, often suffering heavy losses.

The Mk. VIA still has a multi-sided cupola with view ports, that would later be simplified on the Mk. VIB. The easiest way to recognize the Mk. VIA is by its two-piece louvre covers over the radiator.

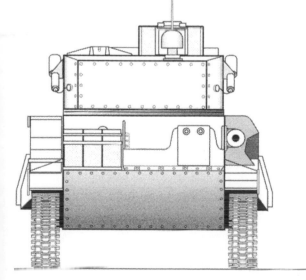

Light Tank Mk. VIB
North Africa, 1940

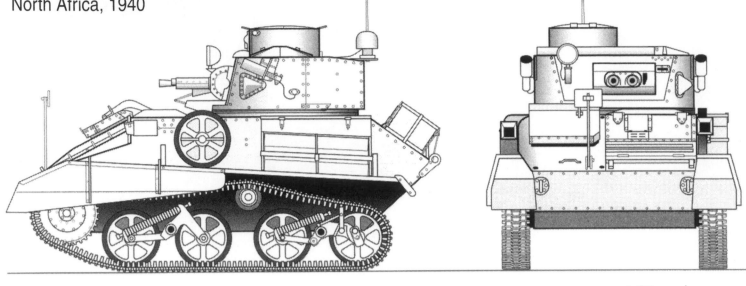

FEET
1:35 scale

0   5   10   15   20

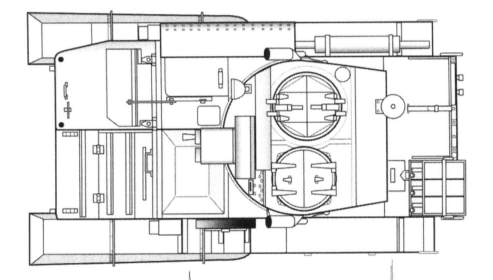

At the outbreak of World War II, the Light Tank Mk. VI was the most numerous tank in service with the British Army. They were used in France in 1940, where their shortcomings were soon recognized. However, after Dunkirk they were still the main tank on the homefront and abroad.

In 1938 the 1st (Light) Battalion returned to Egypt equipped with Mk. VIAs and VIBs, which eventually ended up fed into the early 7th Armoured Division in 1940. In June 1940 there were still 135 in use with 7th AD. These Vickers-Armstrong light tanks were intended for reconnaissance duties by then. However, because of the total lack of tanks in Egypt, they were forced into the "cruiser tank" role as well, often suffering heavy losses.

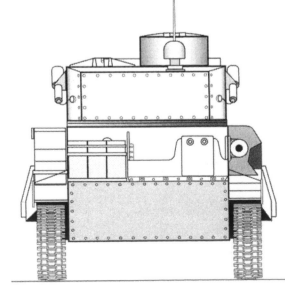

The Cruiser tank, Mark V, was also designated as A13 Mk. III, and as such never really went into battle,
but was ultimately used as a training vehicle back in Britain mainly because of problems connected with the engine cooling system.

Cruiser Tank Mk. V**
Covenanter III (A13 Mk. III**)

There were four versions of the Covenanter: Mark I, II, III and IV.

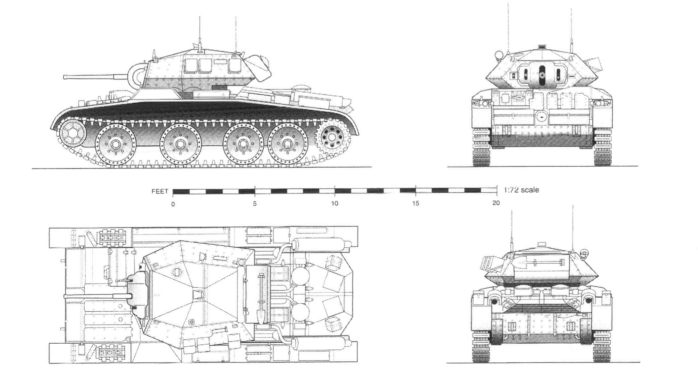

FEET
0   5   10   15   20   1:72 scale

Cruiser Tank Mk. V**
Covenanter III (A13 Mk. III**)

There were four versions of the
Covenanter: Mark I, II, III and IV.

The Covenanter was the further attempt
to utilize the Christie suspension.
Although production reached 1,771
vehicles, very few if any ever saw action,
other than as training vehicles in England
and possibly the Middle East, and a
number were converted to bridgelayers.

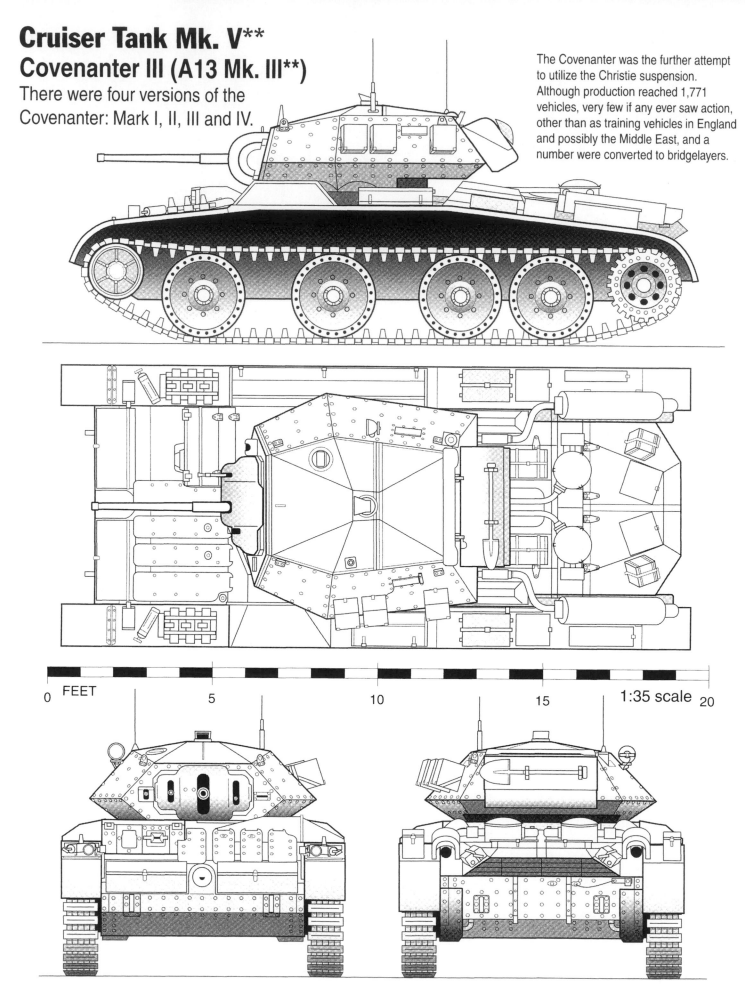

0 FEET   5   10   15   1:35 scale 20

Humber, Light Recon Car, Mk. III
(Car, 4x4, Light Reconnaissance, Humber, Mk. III)

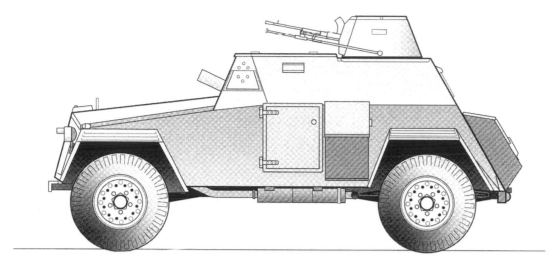

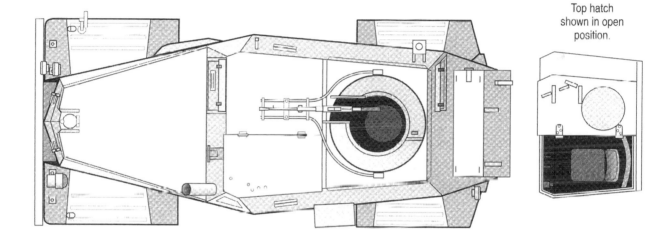

Top hatch shown in open position.

FEET

1:35 scale

0   5   10   15   20

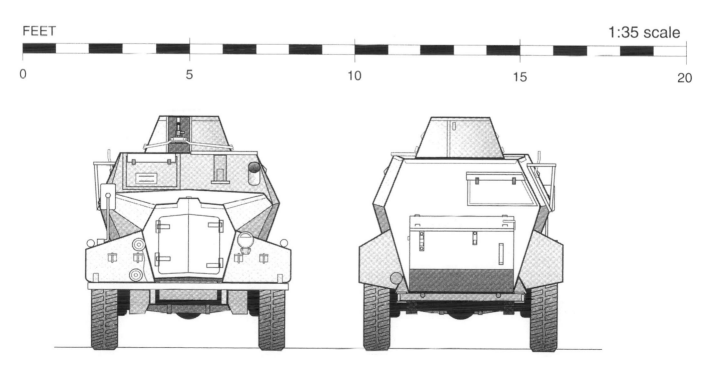

Cruiser Tank Mk. VI
Crusader I (A15)
early

This Mk. I displays the early internal mantlet, but the late Crusader I was also fitted with the bulbous external mantlet of the Mk. II, and many had their auxiliary MG turret removed as well. The very early wheel covers have been discarded here.

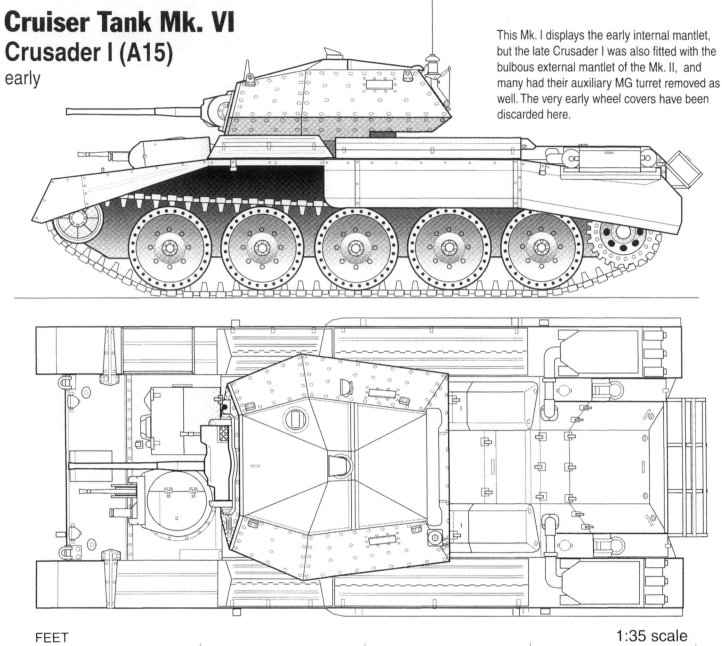

FEET

1:35 scale

0   5   10   15   20

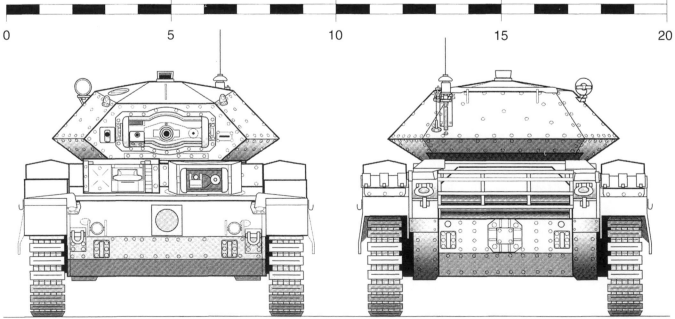

An early Crusader Mk. I, probably disabled by mechanical problems, is being inspected by Afrika Korps troops.
It features the early headlamps, small MG turret, early mantlet, and wheel covers.

A nice top view of the Crusader II with the later mantlet, and still retaining its little MG turret, but with the later style headlamp position and guards.

Cruiser Tank Mk. VIA
Crusader II (A15)

The Crusader II still featured the auxiliary MG turret, but it was often phased out in the field.

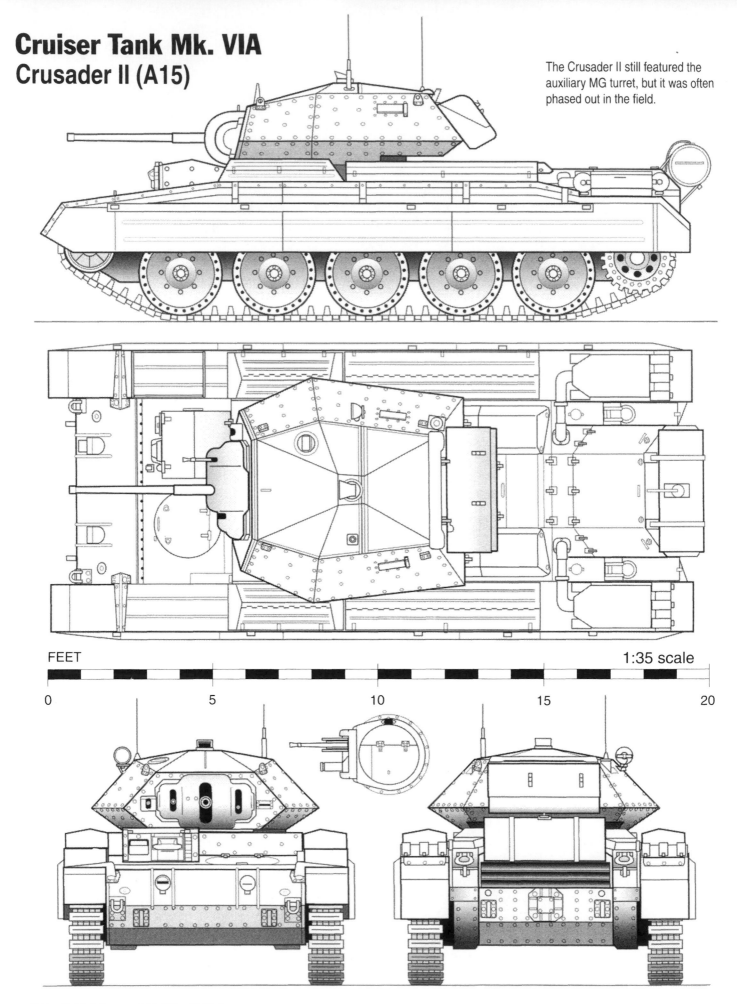

FEET

1:35 scale

0   5   10   15   20

Carrier, Bren No. 2 Mk. I

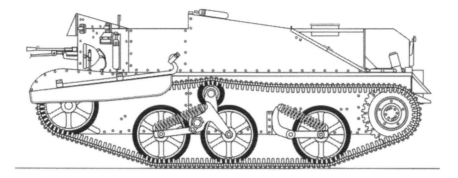

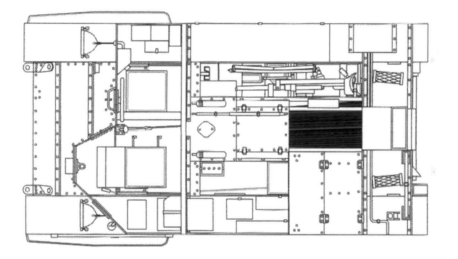

FEET

1:35 scale

0   5   10   15   20

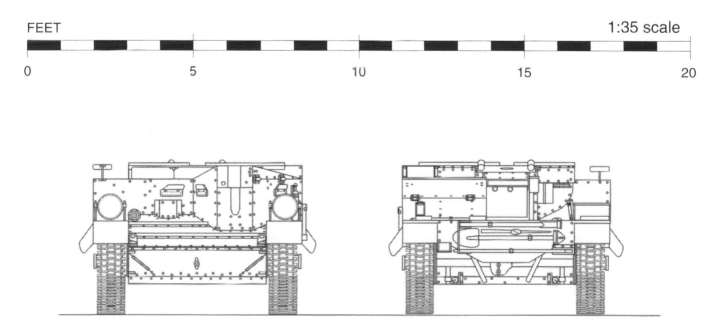

Beaverette Mk. III,
Light Reconnaissance Car

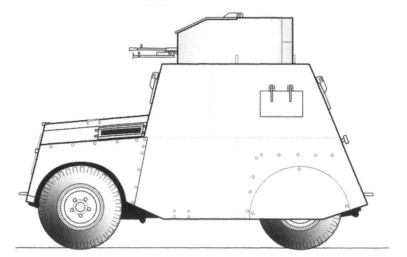

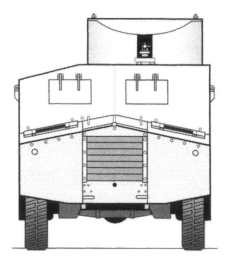

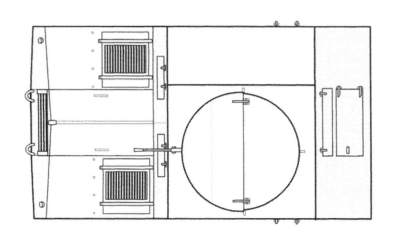

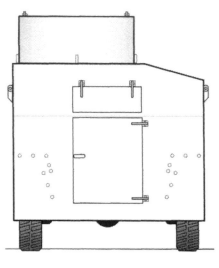

FEET

1:35 scale

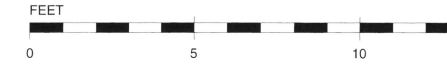

0   5   10   15   20

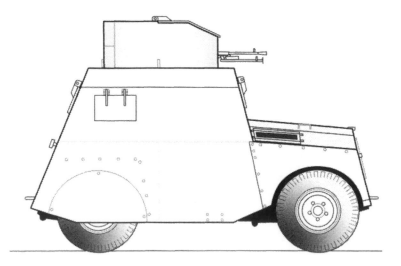

The "Car, 4 x 2, Light Reconnaissance, Standard Mark III, Beaverette III" was one af a series of light armored cars pressed into service for home defense units, shortly after the Dunkirk evacuation and the threat of invasion by Germany.

The name derives from the fact that Lord Beaverbrook was eager to have defense vehicles to protect the vital aircraft factories, because it would be the British air force that would have to stop the invasion.

The Beaverette I and II were both open-topped vehicles, but the III and IV were roofed in with a turret on top. A grand total of 2,800 of all four Marks were built and used by both the Army and the R.A.F. They were lightly armored with mild steel plates and even 3" oak planking reinforcing the frontal armor from behind. The Beaverette III (also known as "Beaverbug I") was fully enclosed and with proper armor plate.

Beaverettes mounted either a Bren light MG, or later-turreted versions had twin Vickers "K" type aircraft-type MGs.

Humber Scout Car, Mk. I

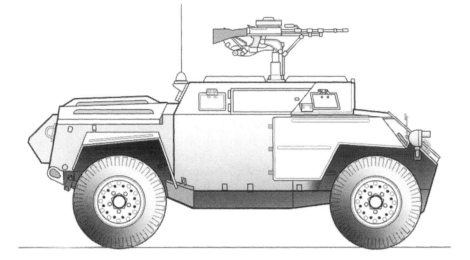

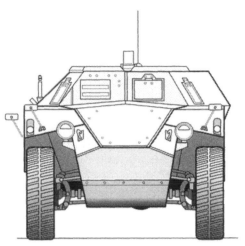

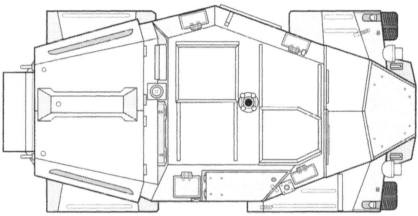

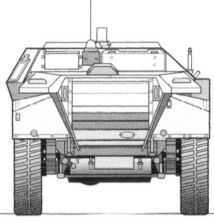

FEET

1:35 scale

0   5   10   15   20

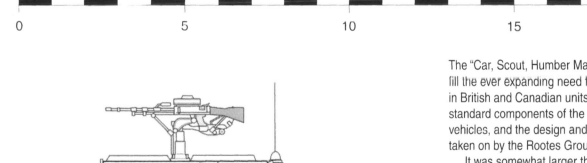

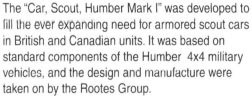

The "Car, Scout, Humber Mark I" was developed to fill the ever expanding need for armored scout cars in British and Canadian units. It was based on standard components of the Humber 4x4 military vehicles, and the design and manufacture were taken on by the Rootes Group.

It was somewhat larger than the Daimler Dingo and could accommodate a crew of three, rather than two. The fixed roof featured two sliding hatches, and mounted a remote-control Bren light machine gun which could be operated from inside the vehicle. The Mark II version was the same configuration but slightly heavier, and with synchromesh gear improvements.

The Humber Scout Car saw heavy useage in many Canadian and British armored regiments in their various headquarters troops.

Grant I,
Cruiser Tank

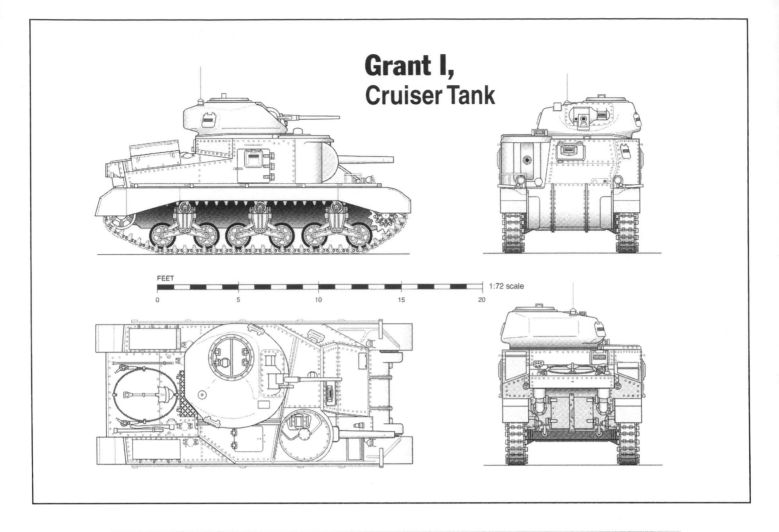

FEET
1:72 scale
0   5   10   15   20

At the Heliopolis repair depot near Cairo, Egypt, a row of damaged Grants and Lees have had their ammunition and gear removed as a safety factor during repairs, January 1943.

Grant I, Cruiser Tank

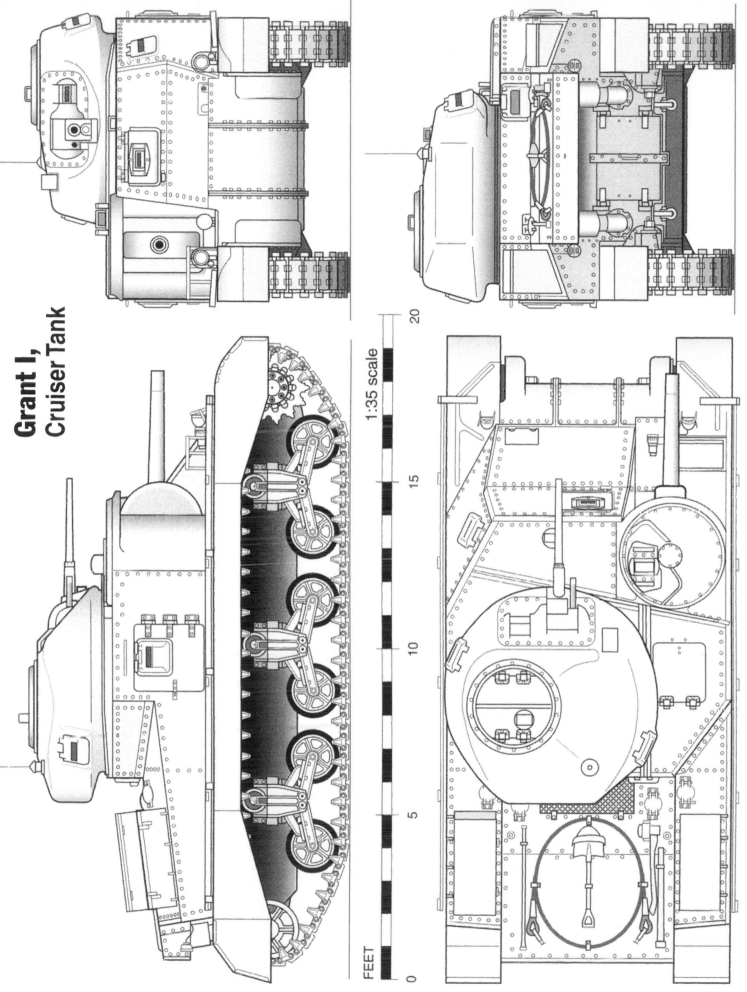

1:35 scale

FEET

0   5   10   15   20

Grant I, Cruiser Tank

The American M3 medium tank
built for British service,
North Africa, 1942

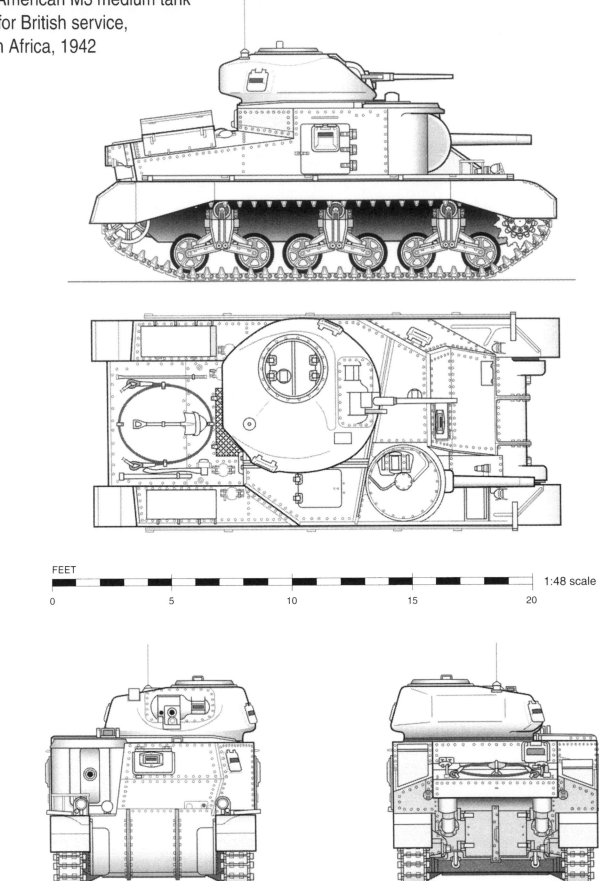

FEET

0   5   10   15   20

1:48 scale

General Montgomery atop a Grant tank as he inspects the forward positions of the British lines in Libya, late December 1942.

Eighth Army Grants moving at speed in their advance toward Tripoli, Tunisia, January 27, 1943.

Stuart I (Honey)
Light Tank M3 (early production)

1:35 Scale

15

10

5

FEET

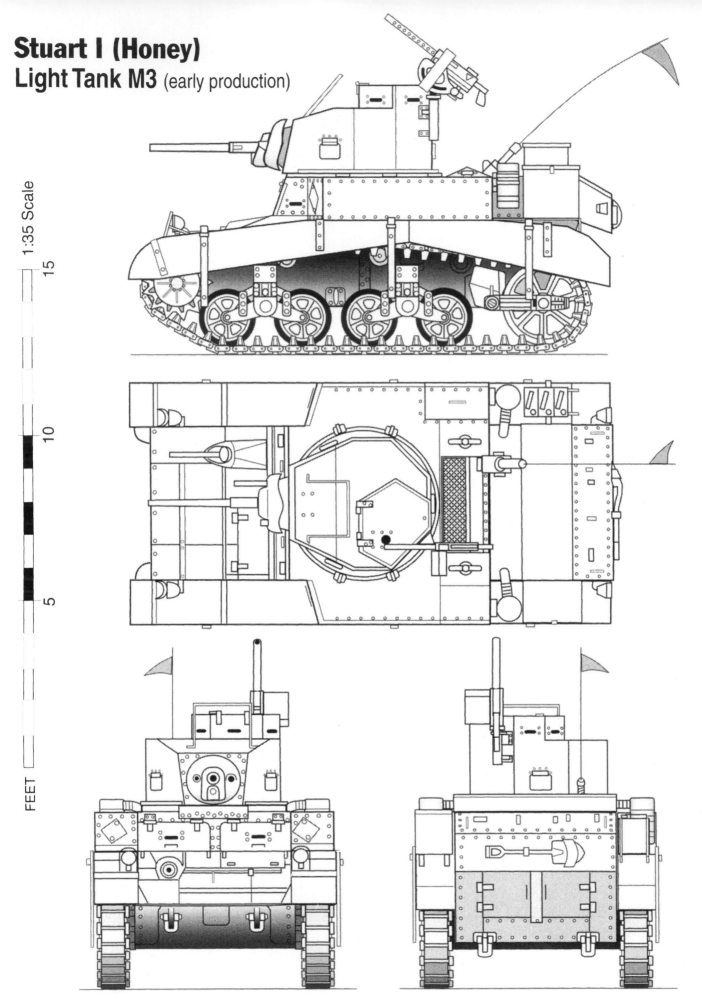

This British 7th Armoured Division crew of a newly arrived American M3 (Honey) light tank
mount their vehicle in preparation to move forward into combat.

Above is a troop of Honeys moving at speed through the desert.

Once the British experienced German air attacks in France, they were quick to develop a light tank, AA Mk. I on the Mk. VIA chassis, soon to be followed by another light tank, AA Mk. II on the Mk. VIB chassis. Here we see a Mk. I being shown off to dignitaries in Britain, and below, a Mk. II in the desert being loaded onto a transporter.

Light Tank, AA Mk. II
North Africa, 1942

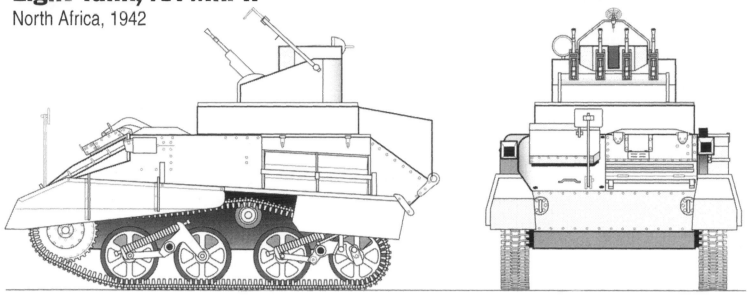

FEET

0   5   10   15   20

1:35 scale

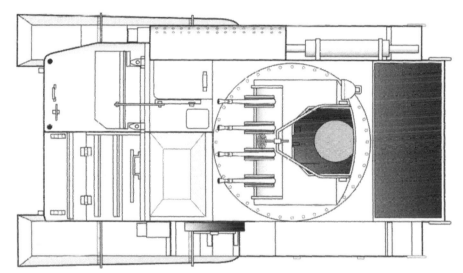

The effect of German air power in France and the Low Countries during May 1940 led to the hasty development of AA tanks to counter this threat. A number of Mk. VIA and VIB light tanks of the day were soon modified to mount a small power-operated turret fitted with four 7.92mm Besa machine guns in tandem.

Soon four of these AA tanks were integrated into the regimental HQ squadron of each British armored regiment. The early model was designated Tank, Light, AA Mk. I on the VIA chassis. This was superceded by Tank, Light, AA Mk. II built on the VIB chassis. It had minor improvements to the turret, an improved sighting arrangement, and extra stowage space in the rear. They were first used operationally in North Africa.

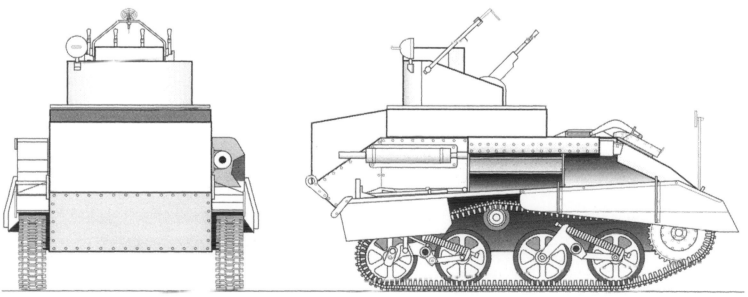

AEC "Dorchester"
Armored Command Vehicle

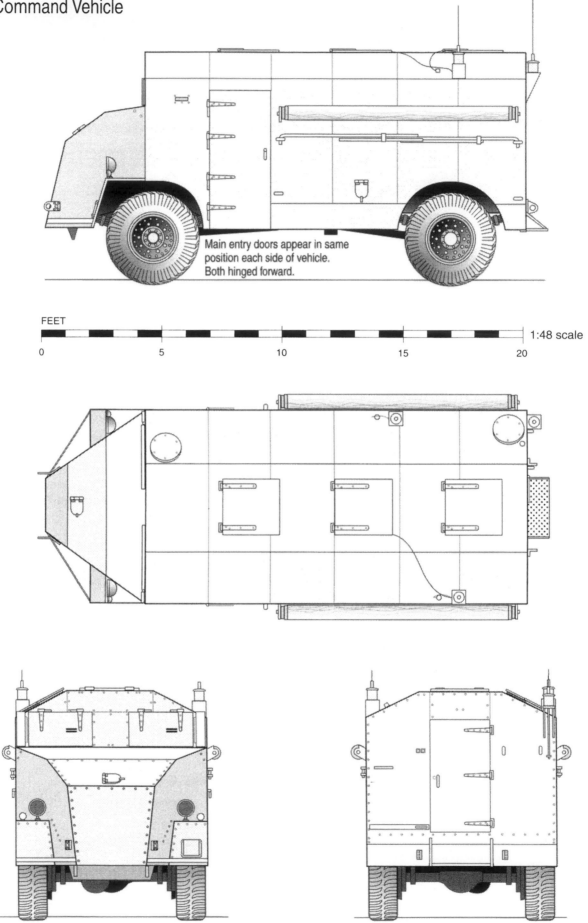

Main entry doors appear in same position each side of vehicle. Both hinged forward.

FEET

0   5   10   15   20

1:48 scale

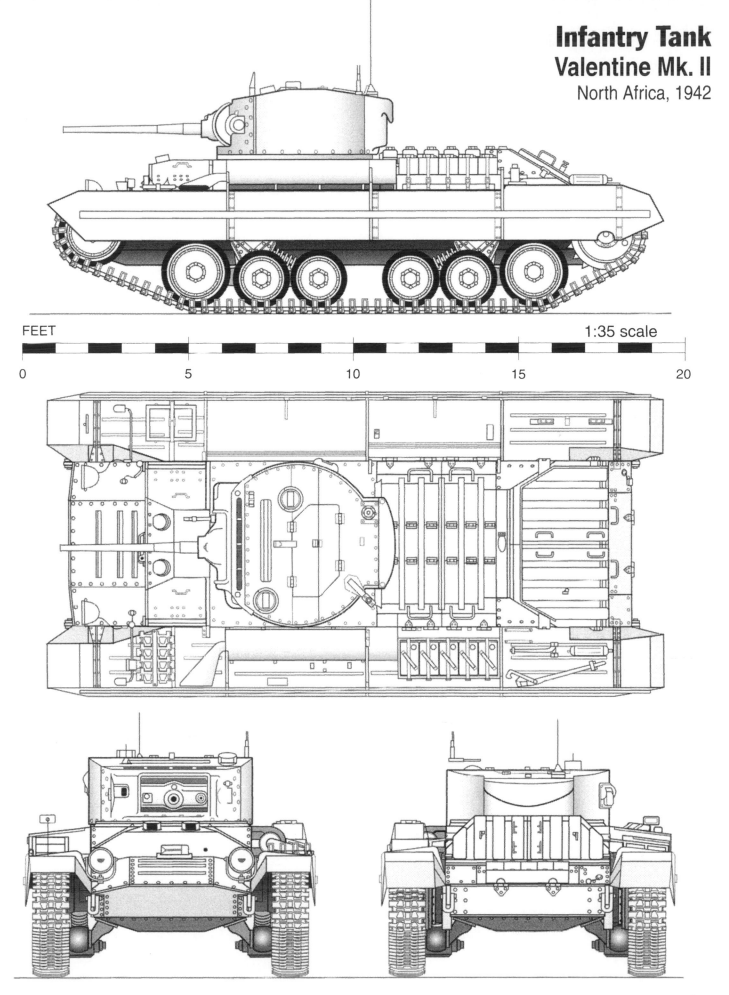

Infantry Tank
Valentine Mk. II
North Africa, 1942

FEET

1:35 scale

0   5   10   15   20

Infantry Tank, Mk. IIA* (A12)
Matilda, Mk. IV
(late production)

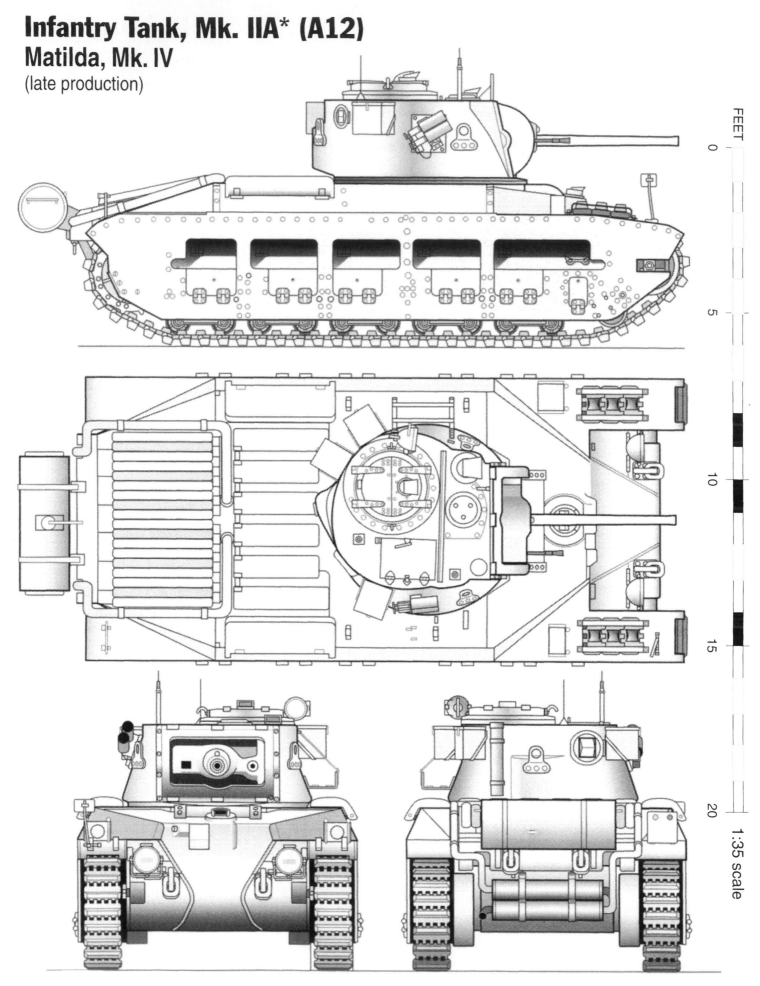

FEET

0

5

10

15

20

1:35 scale

Armored Car, Daimler Mk. 1

Production of the Daimler armored car reached 2,694, of all marks. Upon arrival in North Africa the Mk. I's were soon fitted with a spare wheel on the left side. The main users of the Daimler a/cars in Africa were 11th Hussars, who received them in February 1943, and the 12th Royal Lancers got theirs in March 1943. The Daimler could drive forward or reverse at equal speeds.

These vehicles were very popular with their crews, and in Italy in the summer of 1944 when the King's Dragoon Guards were to be issued Staghounds to replace their old Daimlers, they protested so vigorously that they were allowed to overhaul and keep them. The Mk. I displays the early gun mantlet which was upgraded in the Mk. II.

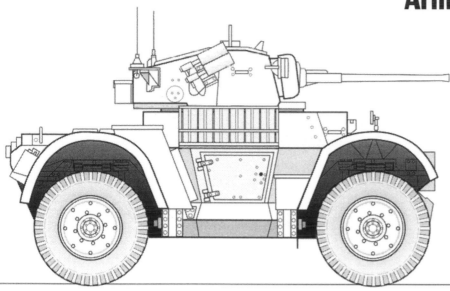

FEET

0   5   10   15   20

1:35 scale

Self-Propelled 25-pdr "Bishop"

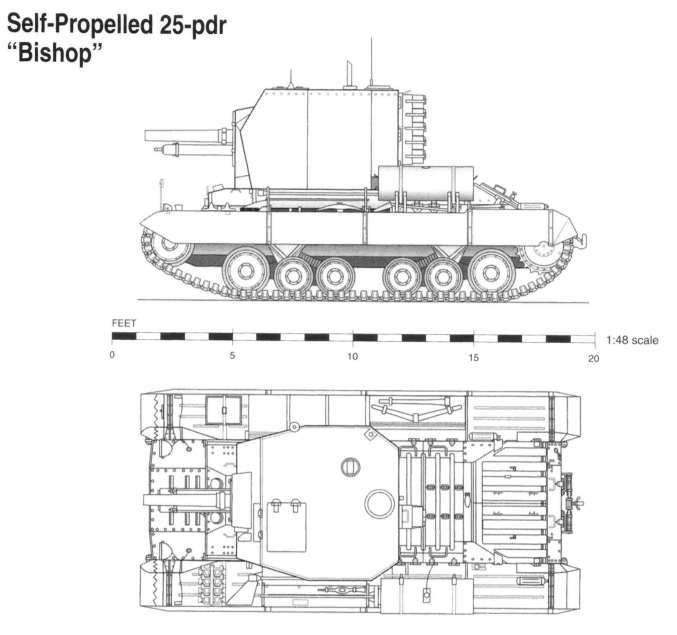

FEET

0   5   10   15   20

1:48 scale

The "Bishop" was an attempt by the British to adapt their versatile 25-pounder field gun to a self-propelled gun role. The Valentine chassis was chosen, and in mid-June 1941 production was initiated. By November 1941 an order for 100 had been placed, but delays led to these vehicles not arriving in Africa until April 1942, well after the new 6-pounder had already filled its proposed anti-tank role.

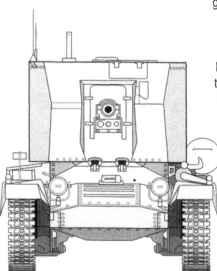

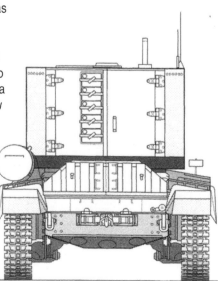

Cruiser Tank Mk. VI
Crusader III (A15)

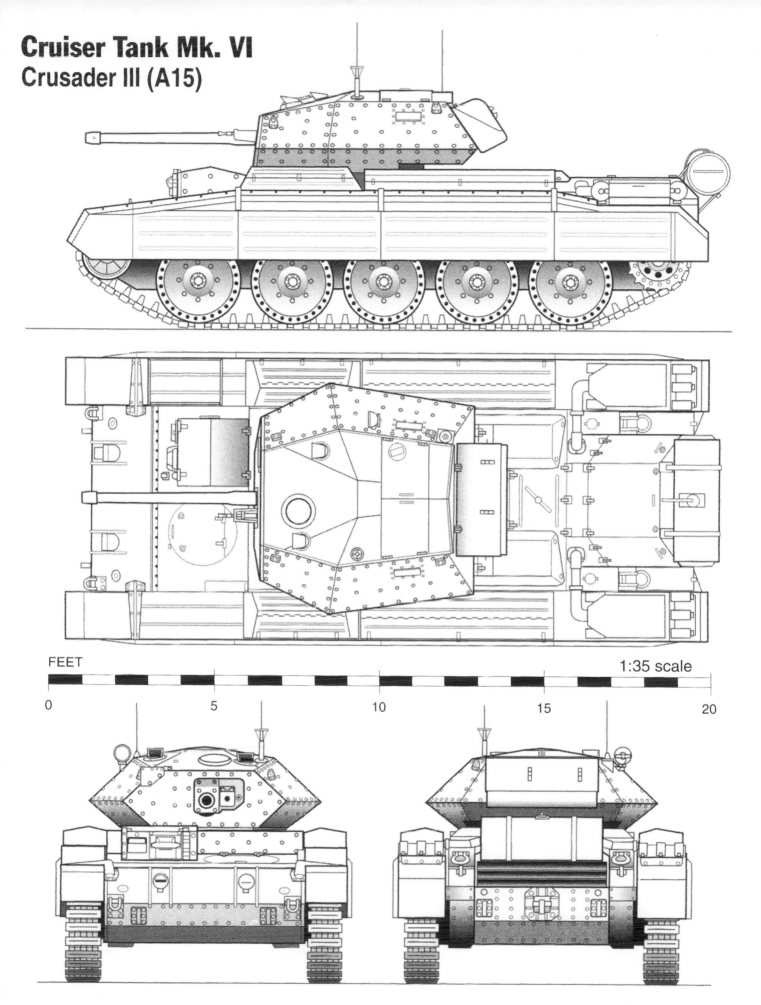

FEET

1:35 scale

0   5   10   15   20

One of the last remaining examples of the Crusader Mk. III, mounting the 6-pounder gun, on display at the Aberdeen Proving Ground.

Cruiser Tank Mk. VI, Crusader III (A15)

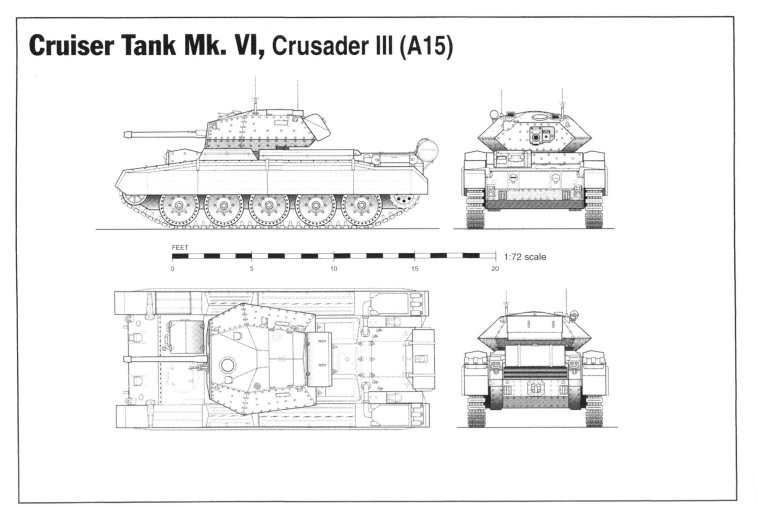

FEET

0   5   10   15   20   1:72 scale

Carrier, AEC, 6pdr Gun, Mk. I
"Deacon"

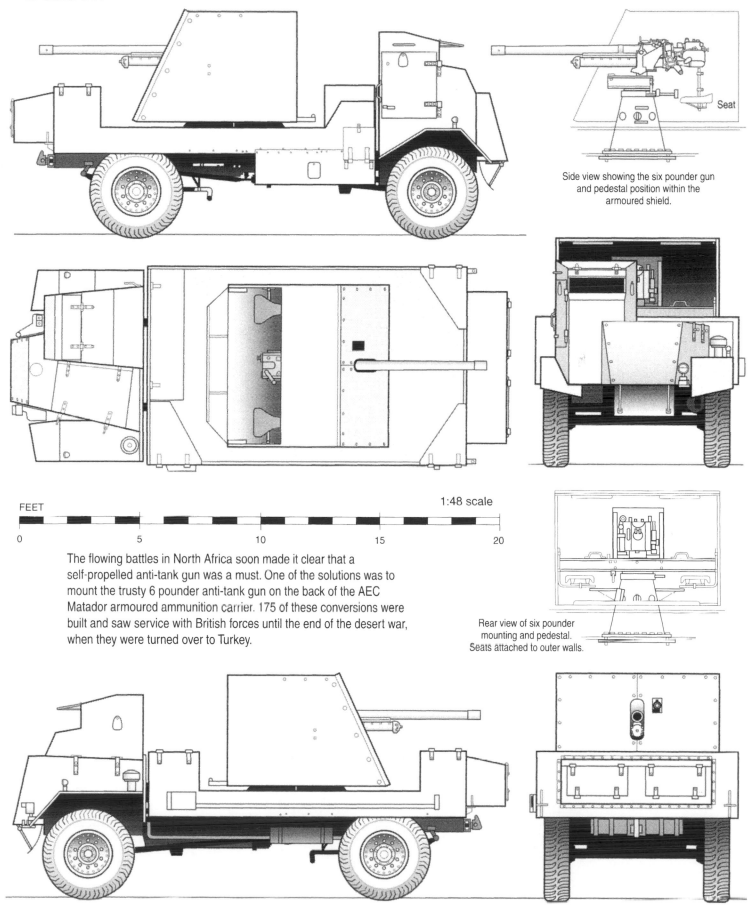

Side view showing the six pounder gun
and pedestal position within the
armoured shield.

FEET

1:48 scale

0   5   10   15   20

The flowing battles in North Africa soon made it clear that a
self-propelled anti-tank gun was a must. One of the solutions was to
mount the trusty 6 pounder anti-tank gun on the back of the AEC
Matador armoured ammunition carrier. 175 of these conversions were
built and saw service with British forces until the end of the desert war,
when they were turned over to Turkey.

Rear view of six pounder
mounting and pedestal.
Seats attached to outer walls.

Seat

Daimler Scout Car Mk. II

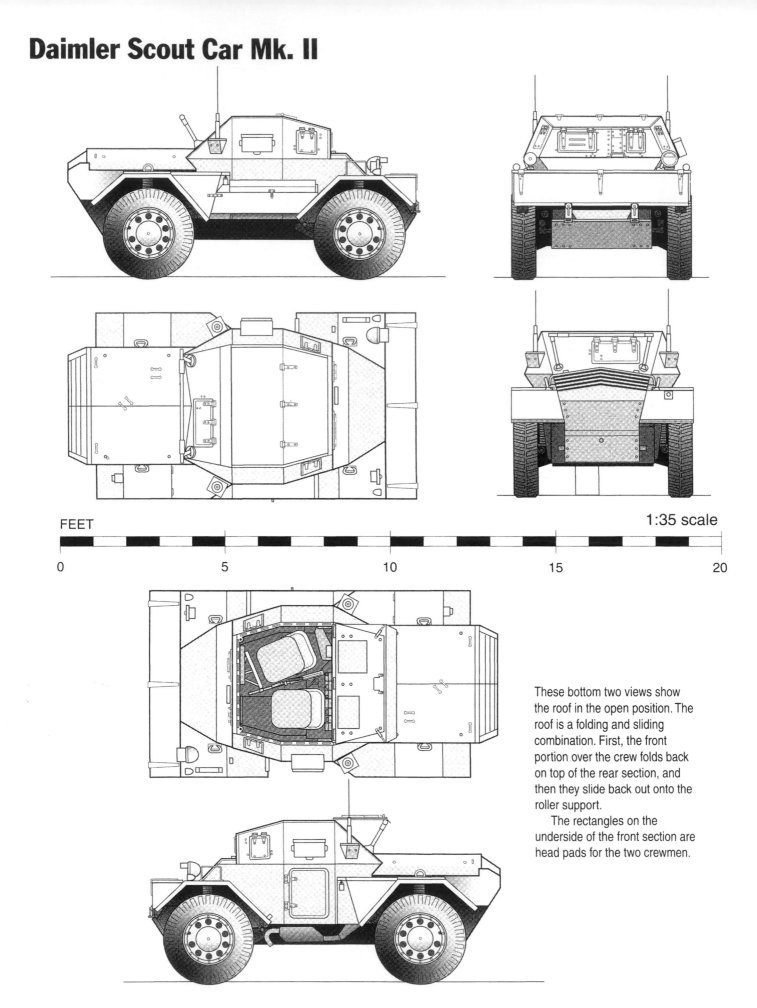

FEET

1:35 scale

0   5   10   15   20

These bottom two views show the roof in the open position. The roof is a folding and sliding combination. First, the front portion over the crew folds back on top of the rear section, and then they slide back out onto the roller support.

The rectangles on the underside of the front section are head pads for the two crewmen.

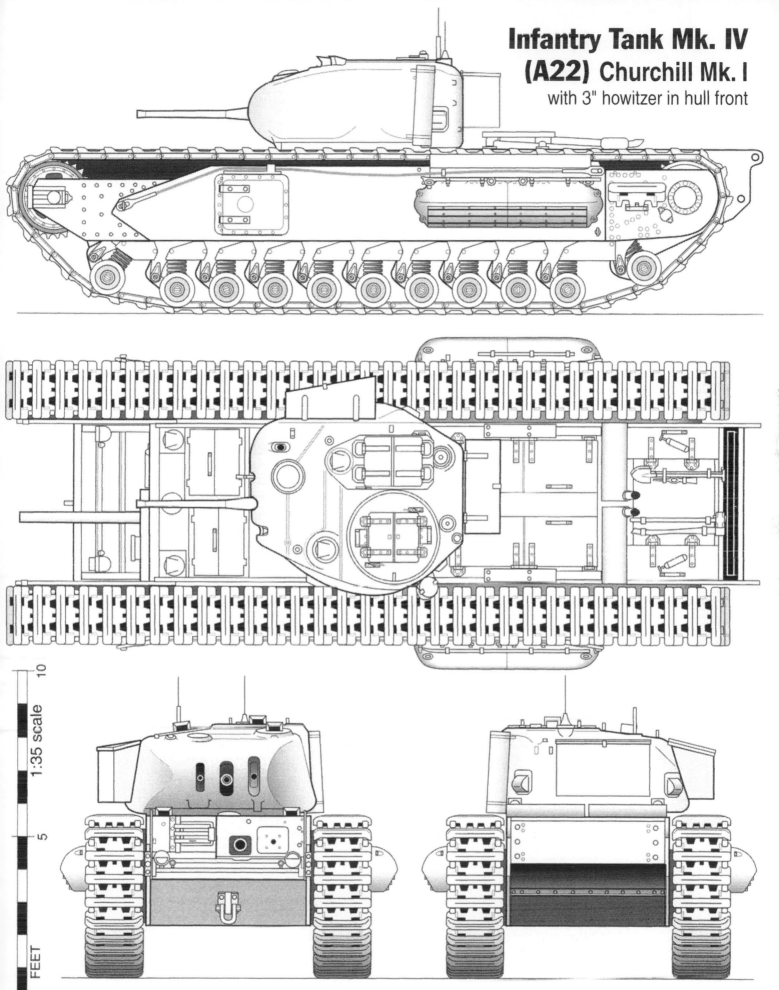

Infantry Tank Mk. IV
(A22) Churchill Mk. I
with 3" howitzer in hull front

1:35 scale

FEET

0   5   10

A Churchill AVRE preparing for an attack near Bretteville-le-Rabet, France, August 14, 1944.
The Churchill AVRE mounted a huge Petard spigot mortar for attacking enemy bunkers and other concrete obstacles.

Another Churchill AVRE shown on the outskirts of St. Aubin-sur-Mer, France, just ashore during the D-Day landings, June 6, 1944.

Churchill AVRE
Carpet Layer Mk. II (Type C)
fitted with Petard spigot mortar and deep wading trunking

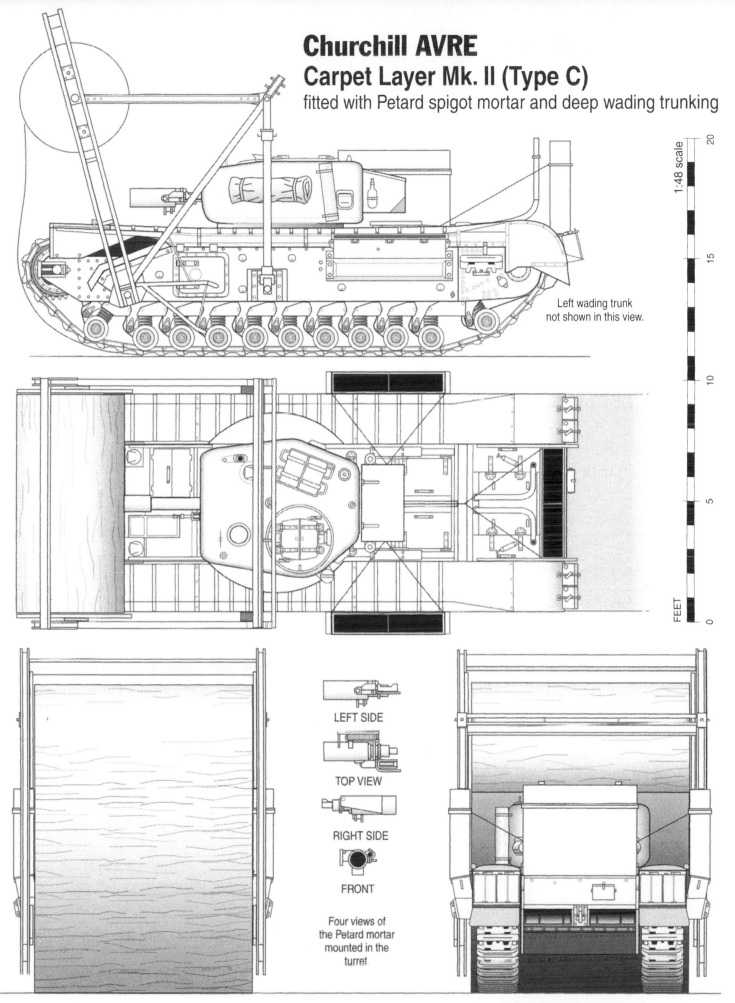

Left wading trunk
not shown in this view.

1:48 scale

FEET

LEFT SIDE

TOP VIEW

RIGHT SIDE

FRONT

Four views of
the Petard mortar
mounted in the
turret

Infantry Tank Mk. IV (A22) Churchill Mk. II
(Upgraded)

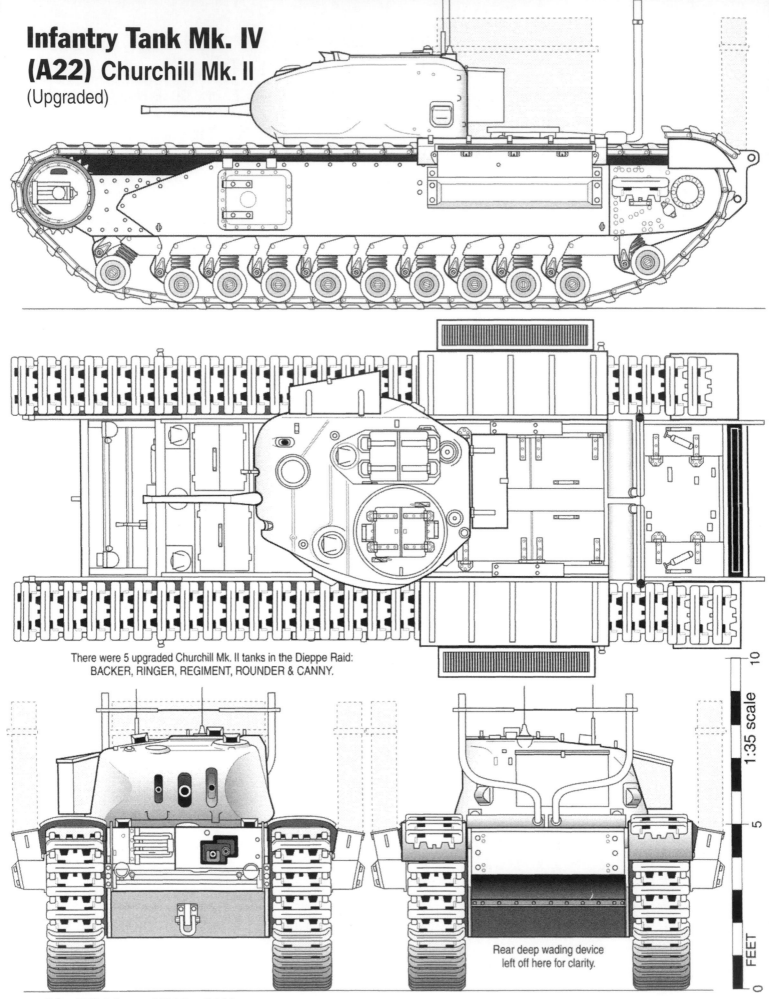

There were 5 upgraded Churchill Mk. II tanks in the Dieppe Raid:
BACKER, RINGER, REGIMENT, ROUNDER & CANNY.

Rear deep wading device
left off here for clarity.

1:35 scale

FEET

10

5

0

Staghound III
(U.S. T17E3)

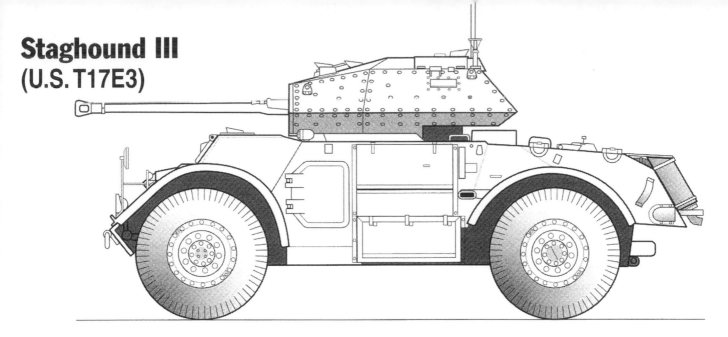

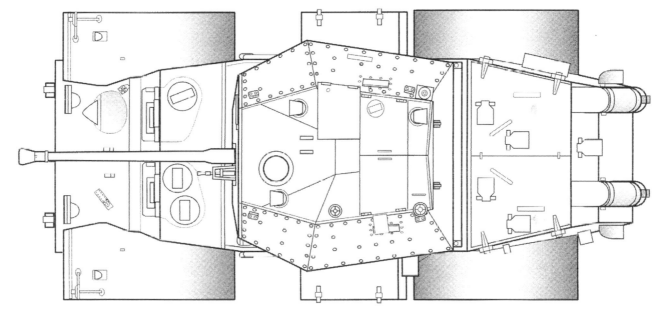

FEET

1:35 scale

0   5   10   15   20

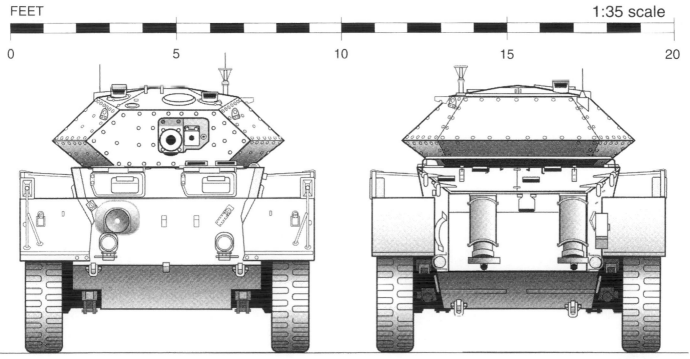

Infantry Tank Valentine
Mk. III

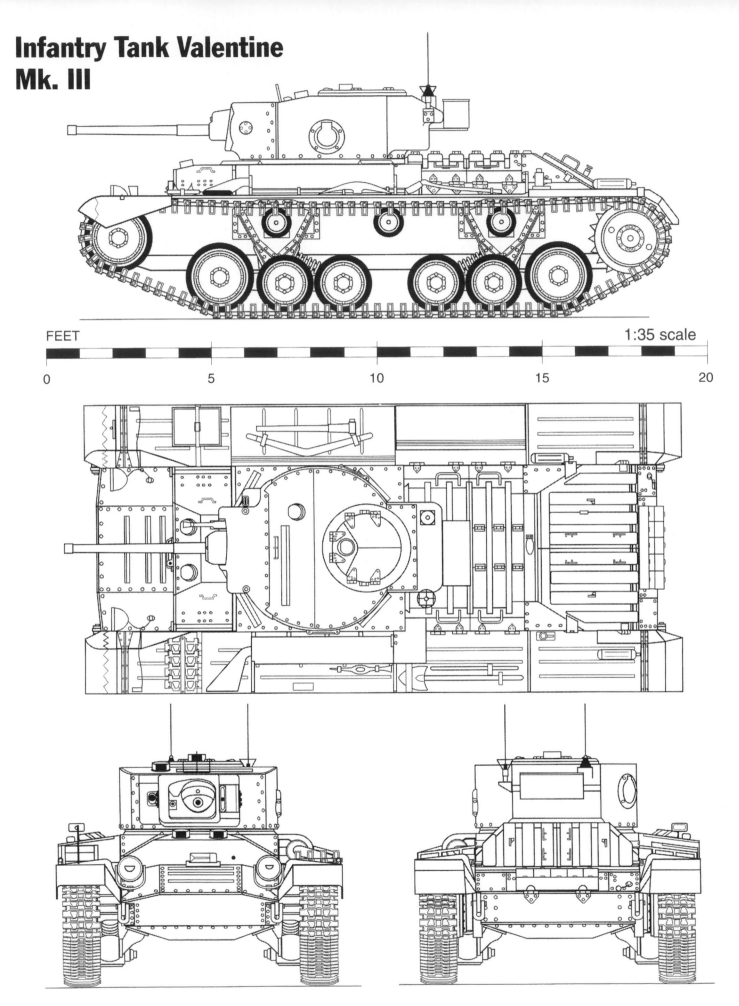

FEET

1:35 scale

0   5   10   15   20

Cruiser Tank, Mk. IV (A27M)
"Cromwell"

The Type D Cromwell hull had an escape hatch added for the hull gunner, and the Type F hull had one added for the driver as well. The optional exhaust flame deflector cowl is shown here, but not on the top and rear views, for the sake of clarity.

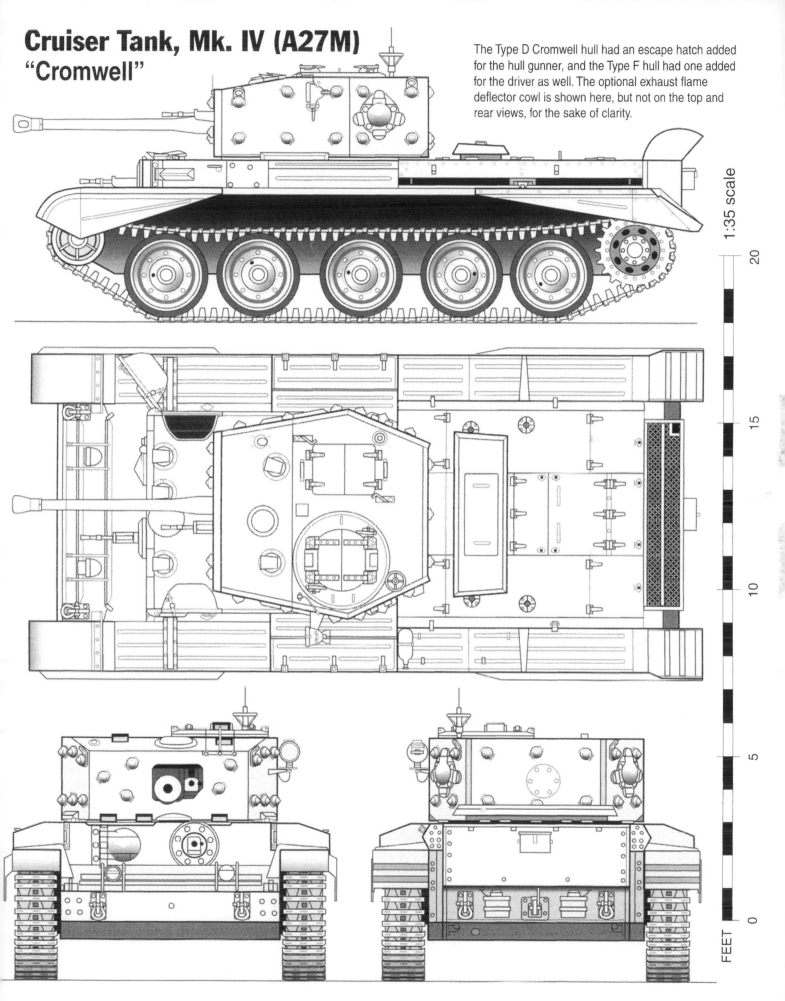

1:35 scale

FEET

A Cromwell IV being put through its traces on the the Bovington test range, launching off a ramp at full speed.

Winston Churchill comes to inspect a Cromwell IV of 2nd Battalion, Armoured Reconnaissance Regiment, of the Guards Armoured Division.
The markings on the nose plate are as follows: the unit number is white 45 on blue over green; yellow 26 in circle is bridge classification weight;
A in white square denotes 2nd Squadron commander's tank; and the red-outlined blue shield with white eye is Guards Armoured Division insignia.

17-pdr Self-Propelled Valentine
"Archer"

The Archer was an attempt to utilize the Valentine chassis for a quickly available S/P 17-pdr. The design, with the gun pointing rearward, solved the problem of the long tube overhang, but created others. The most dreaded of these was the fact that the gun recoil drove the breech mechanism right into the driver's position, thus making it imperative that he was elsewhere during the operation of the gun.

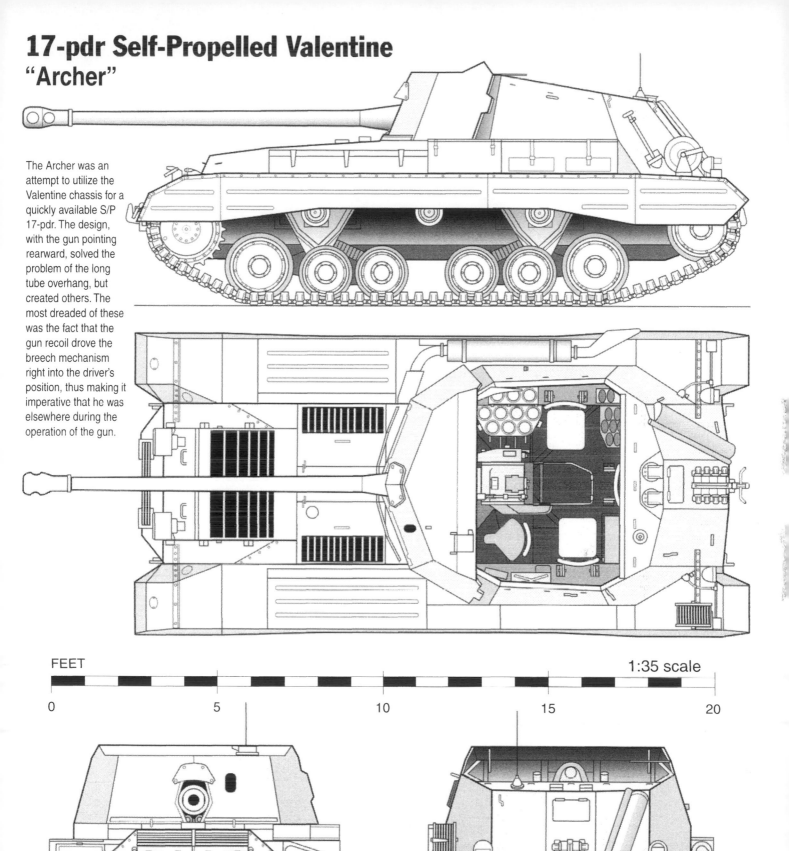

FEET

1:35 scale

0   5   10   15   20

Crusader III, AA Mk. II

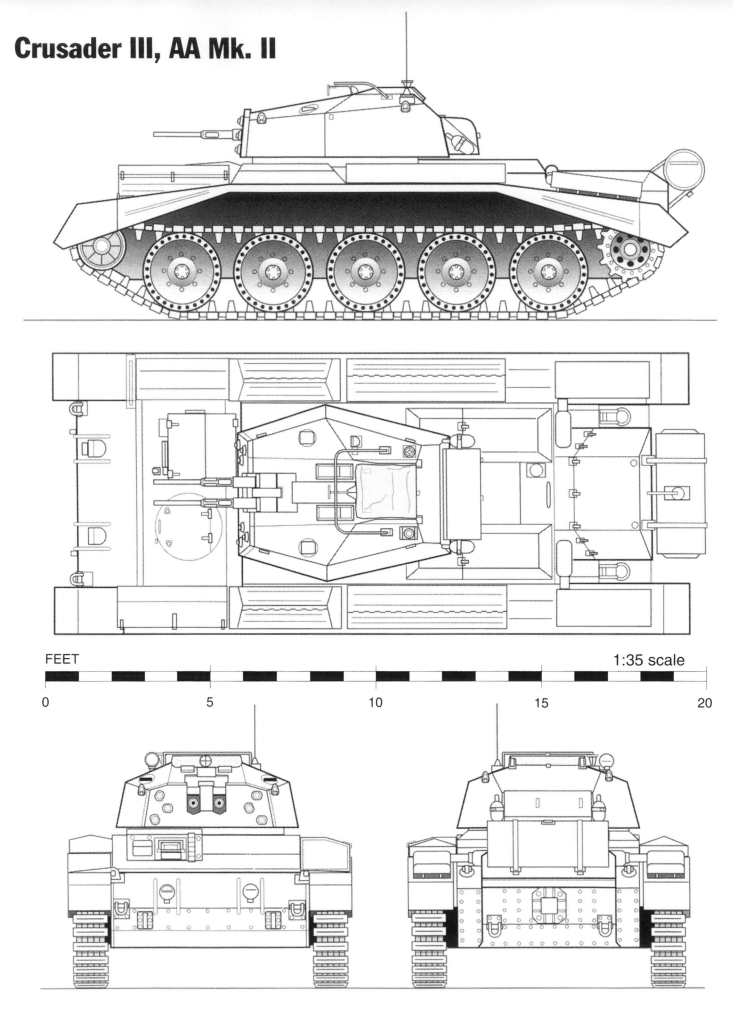

FEET

1:35 scale

0   5   10   15   20

17-pdr, M10, SP "Achilles" IIC Tank Destroyer

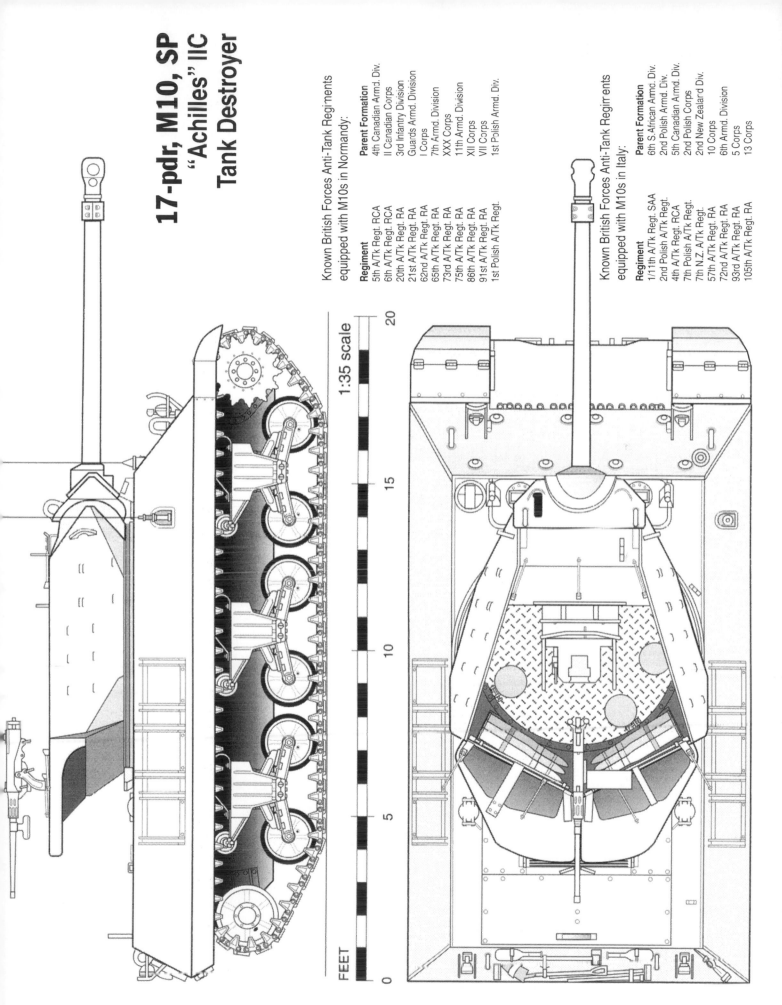

Known British Forces Anti-Tank Regiments equipped with M10s in Normandy:

Regiment	Parent Formation
5th A/Tk Regt. RCA	4th Canadian Armd. Div.
6th A/Tk Regt. RCA	II Canadian Corps
20th A/Tk Regt. RA	3rd Infantry Division
21st A/Tk Regt. RA	Guards Armd. Division
62nd A/Tk Regt. RA	I Corps
65th A/Tk Regt. RA	7th Armd. Division
73rd A/Tk Regt. RA	XXX Corps
75th A/Tk Regt. RA	11th Armd. Division
86th A/Tk Regt. RA	XII Corps
91st A/Tk Regt. RA	VII Corps
1st Polish A/Tk Regt.	1st Polish Armd. Div.

Known British Forces Anti-Tank Regiments equipped with M10s in Italy:

Regiment	Parent Formation
1/11th A/Tk Regt. SAA	6th S. African Armd. Div.
2nd Polish A/Tk Regt.	2nd Polish Armd. Div.
4th A/Tk Regt. RCA	5th Canadian Armd. Div.
7th Polish A/Tk Regt.	2nd Polish Corps
7th N.Z. A/Tk Regt.	2nd New Zealand Div.
57th A/Tk Regt. RA	10 Corps
72nd A/Tk Regt. RA	6th Armd. Division
93rd A/Tk Regt. RA	5 Corps
105th A/Tk Regt. RA	13 Corps

FEET 0 5 10 15 20

1:35 scale

17-pdr, M10, SP
"Achilles" IIC, Tank Destroyer

Much confusion has surfaced trying to establish the actual DTD (Department of Tank Development) designation for this vehicle. The latest research suggests that the whole M10 family was labeled with the code name "Achilles". The M10s with the early V-type turret counterweights were code-named Achilles I, and those with later Duck-Billed counterweights were coded Achilles II. The 17-pdr M10s were then code-named Achilles IC and IIC. The "C" designated the 17-pdr armament, of course. They were only designated by turret type as V-Turret and Duck-Bill Turret, since no M10A1s were supplied to Britain via Lend-Lease.

It should also be noted that nobody outside the DTD ever referred to these tank destroyers by the name Achilles, especially not the troops. Throughout the entire British and Commonwealth armies, they were always known as M10s, and qualified by 3-inch or 17-pdr, respectively.

The name "Wolverine" has also been associated with this vehicle, but no solid reference data suggesting its official useage has ever surfaced to date. One thought is that it may have been a term applied to the M10s by Canadian forces, who have a habit of naming vehicles after animals, especially North American animals.

Realizing the need for even more 17-pdr gunned SP vehicles in the field, the British began to rearm their M10s with the 17-pdr Mk. V gun. This was a modified version of their 17-pdr Mk. II gun which was already in production. Two lugs were added to the breech which permitted its installation in the standard 3-inch mount. A special casting was then welded over the gun shield to accommodate the smaller barrel of the 17-pdr. This casting also helped as a counterweight, and an additional counterweight was fitted to the end of the barrel, directly behind the muzzle brake.

The new direct sight telescope required an elongated hole cut in the gun mantlet. The stowage was rearranged, to accommodate 50 rounds of 17-pdr ammunition, with 6 ready rounds on the turret rear wall and 44 stowed in the sponsons.

The Achilles IC was available for the Normandy landings and the IIC was becoming available by the end of 1944. The Allied units in Italy got their first ICs in around October 1944. The Achilles IIC was a deadly anti-tank weapon used by both British and Commonwealth troops in Italy and Europe, and continued in service even after the war with various countries.

One unexpected aspect of the M10 series was that Allied gunners tended to mistake them for German Panthers, and it got so serious that the US 701st TD Bn. started painting large yellow stripes on the turret counterweights as a recognition feature to both air and anti-tank units.

FEET

0   5   10   15   20

1:35 scale

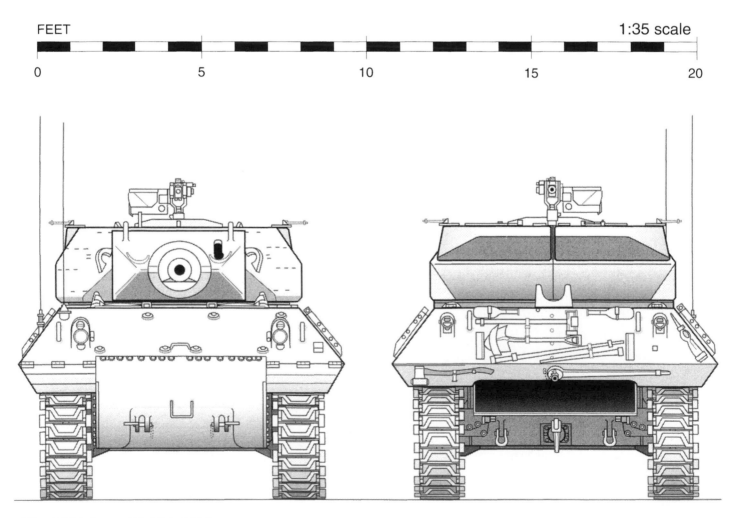

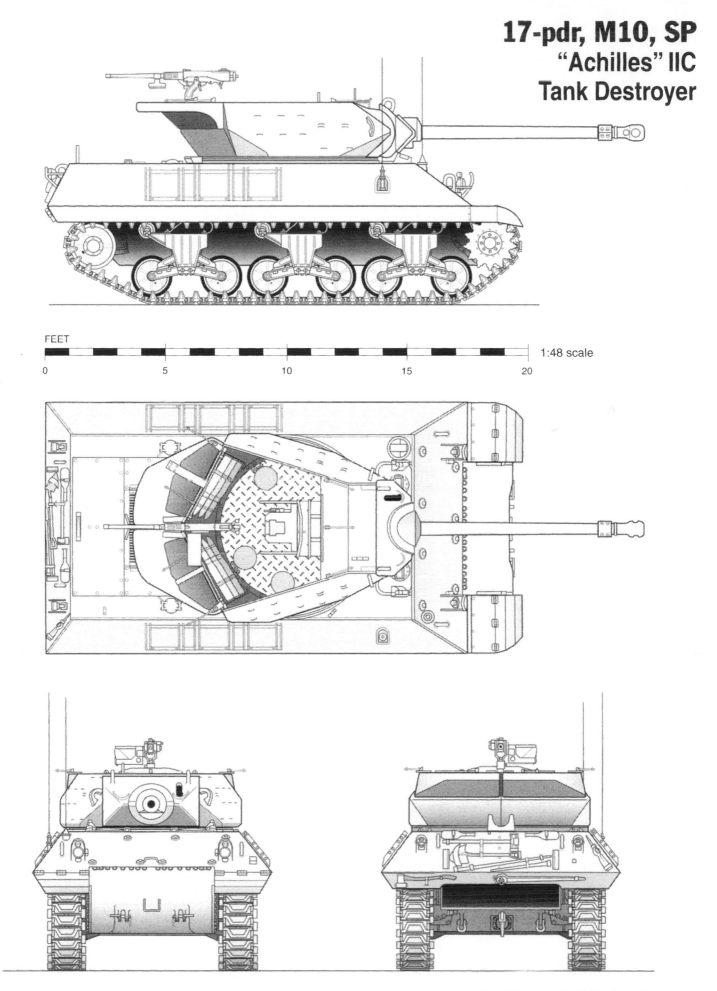

17-pdr, M10, SP
"Achilles" IIC
Tank Destroyer

FEET

0   5   10   15   20

1:48 scale

Armored Car A.E.C. Mk. I

(with Q.F. 2-pounder gun)
North Africa, 1942

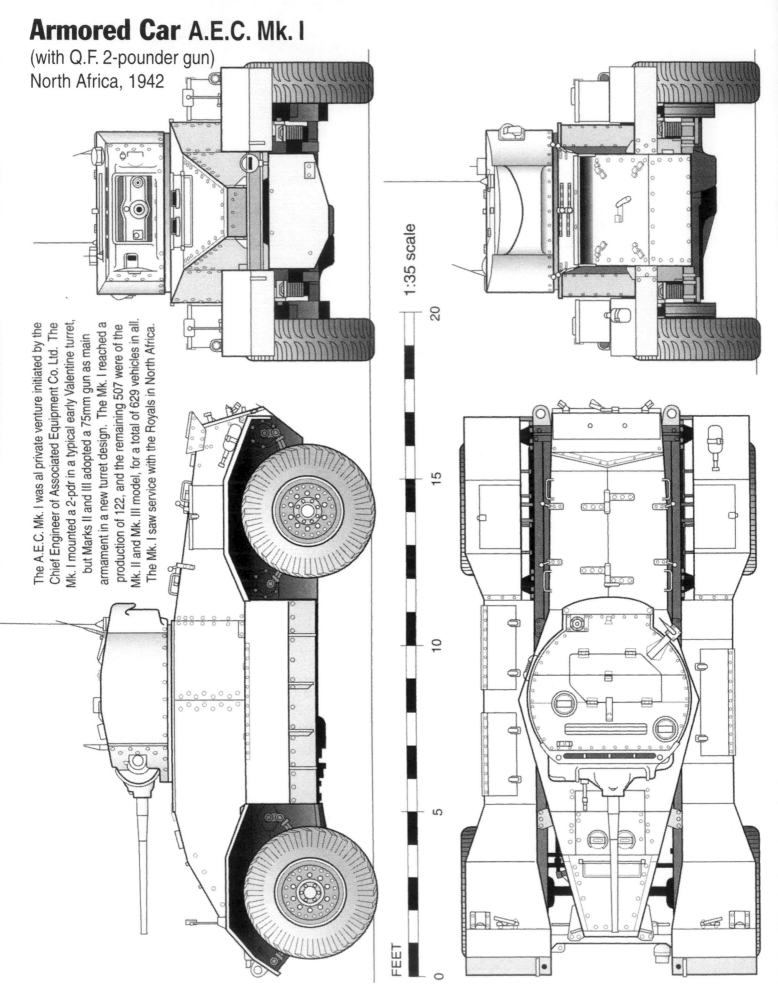

The A.E.C. Mk. I was al private venture initiated by the Chief Engineer of Associated Equipment Co. Ltd. The Mk. I mounted a 2-pdr in a typical early Valentine turret, but Marks II and III adopted a 75mm gun as main armament in a new turret design. The Mk. I reached a production of 122, and the remaining 507 were of the Mk. II and Mk. III model, for a total of 629 vehicles in all. The Mk. I saw service with the Royals in North Africa.

1:35 scale

20

15

10

5

FEET

0

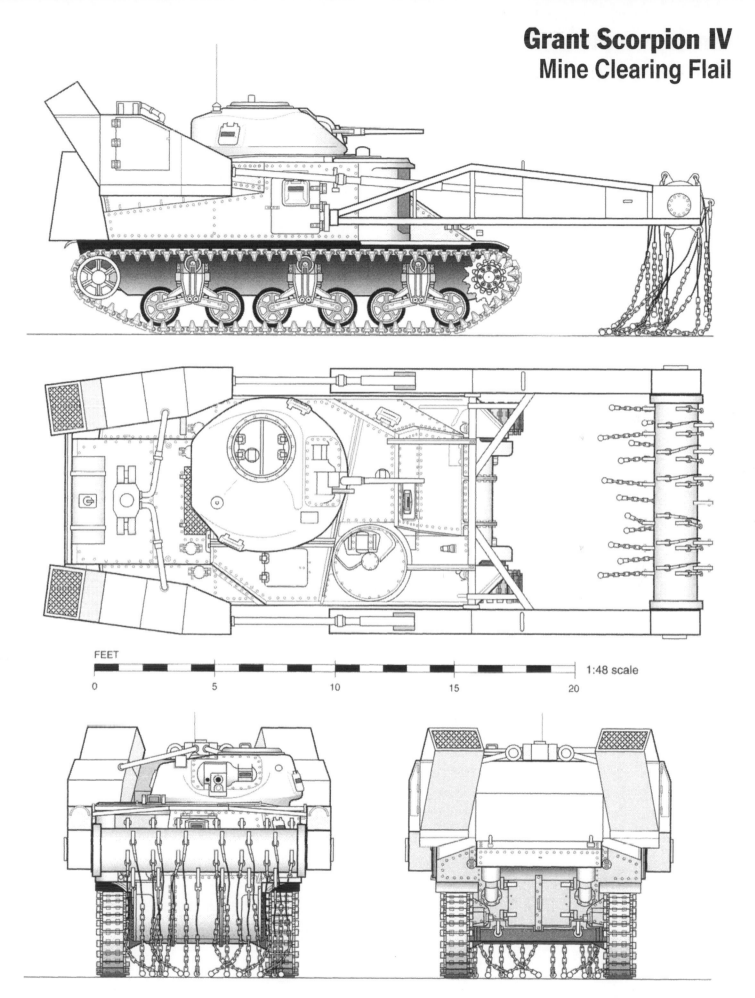

FEET

1:48 scale

0   5   10   15   20

Sherman V, Crab II
Mine Clearance Devise

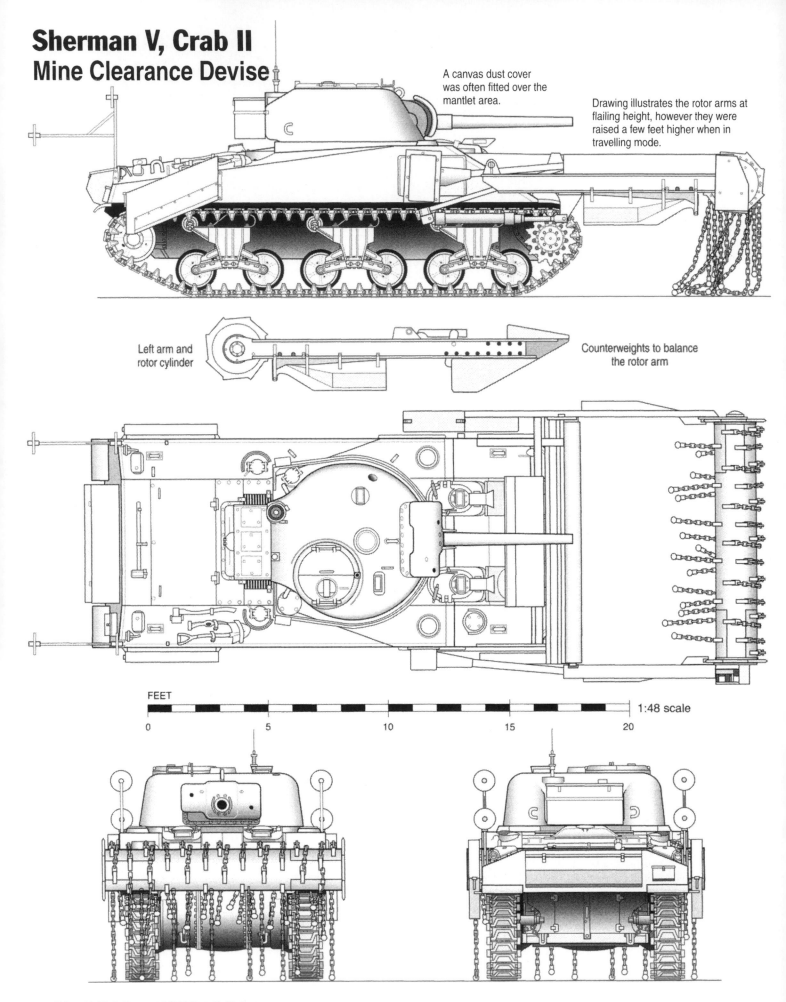

A canvas dust cover was often fitted over the mantlet area.

Drawing illustrates the rotor arms at flailing height, however they were raised a few feet higher when in travelling mode.

Left arm and rotor cylinder

Counterweights to balance the rotor arm

FEET

0   5   10   15   20

1:48 scale

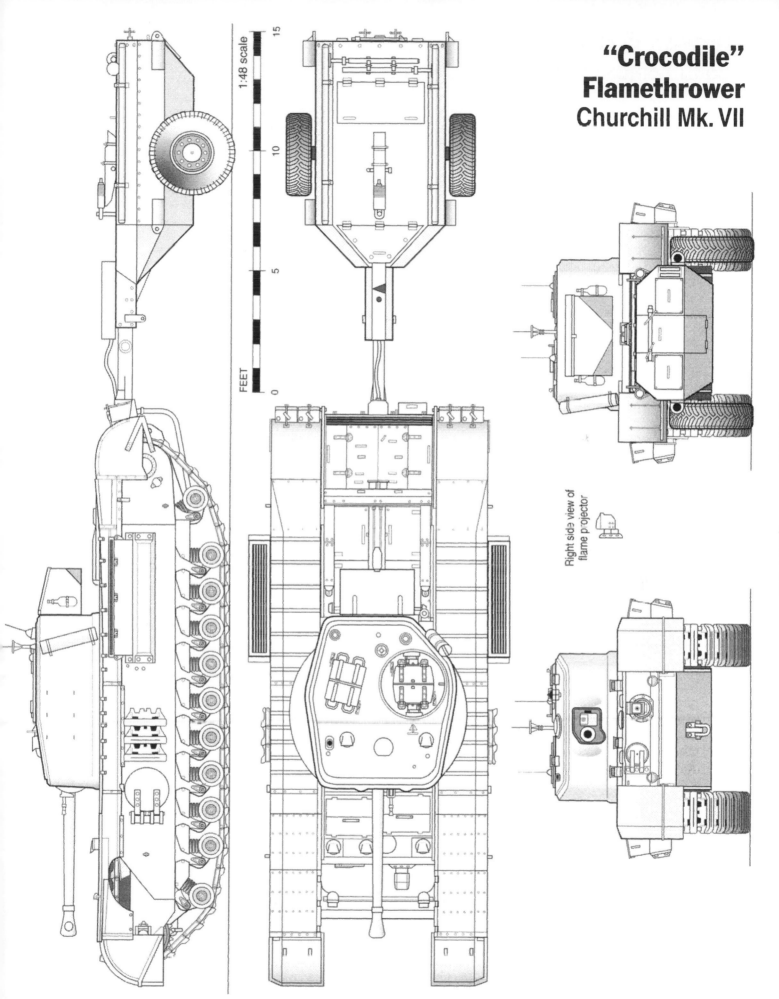

"Crocodile"
Flamethrower
Churchill Mk. VII

1:48 scale

FEET

15

10

5

0

Right side view of
flame projector

Sherman B.A.R.V.
(Beach Armored Recovery Vehicle)

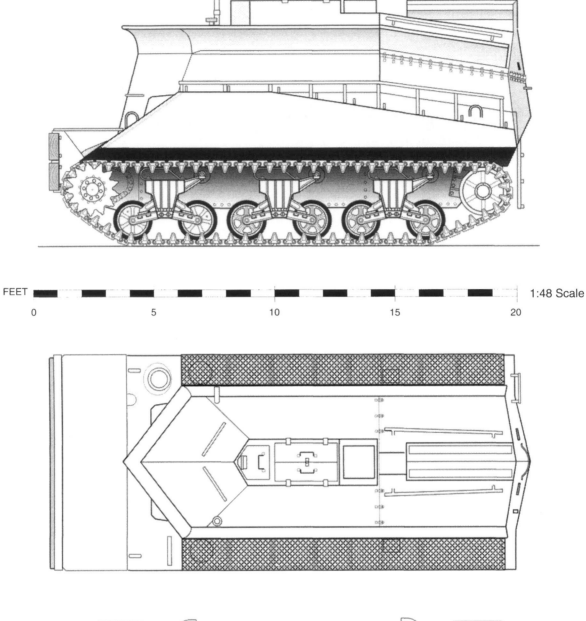

FEET

0   5   10   15   20

1:48 Scale

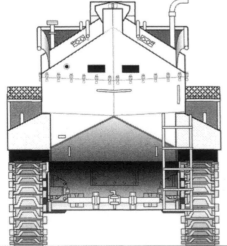

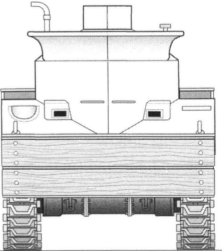

Sherman B.A.R.V.
(Beach Armored Recovery Vehicle)

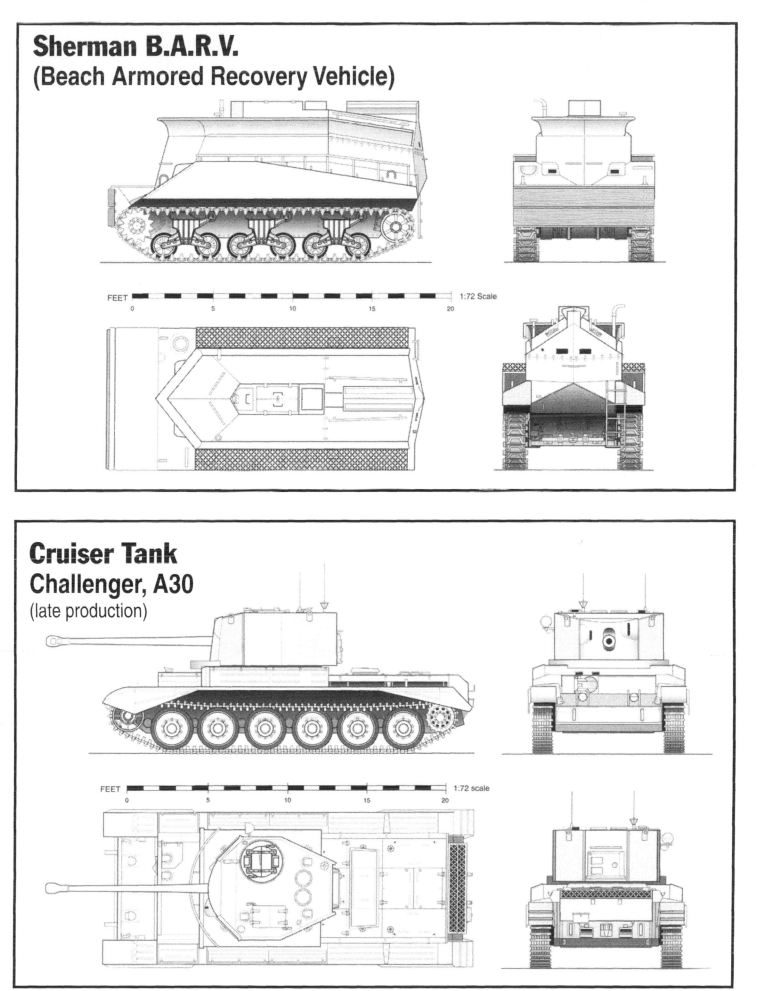

FEET 0 5 10 15 20   1:72 Scale

Cruiser Tank
Challenger, A30
(late production)

FEET 0 5 10 15 20   1:72 scale

Cruiser Tank
Challenger, A30
(late production)

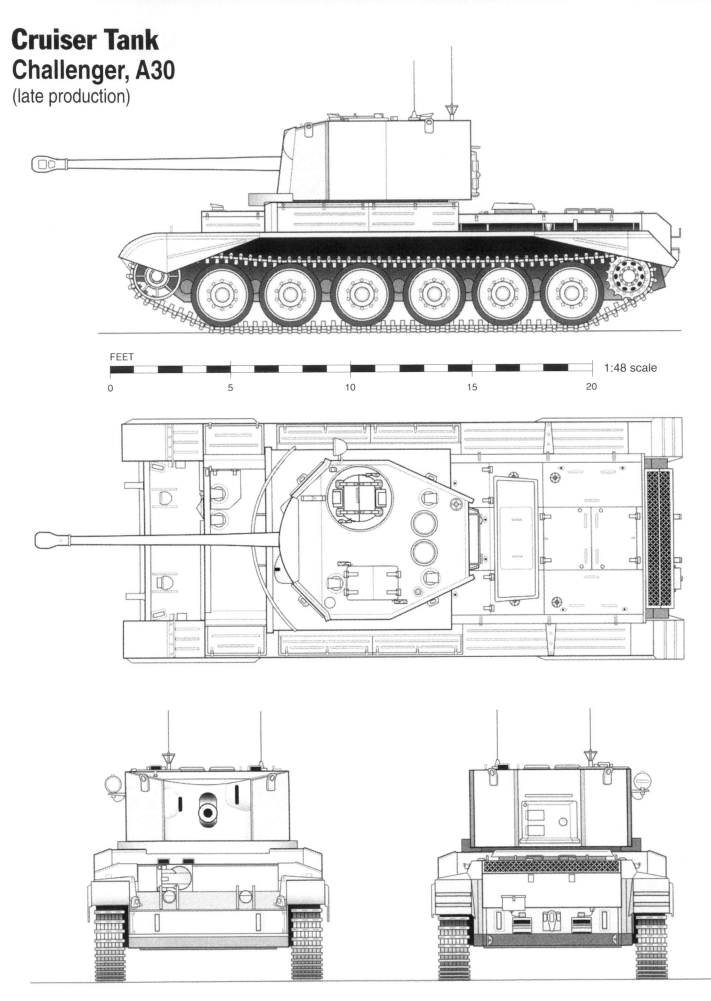

FEET

0   5   10   15   20

1:48 scale

Armored Car
A.E.C. Mk. III
(with Q.F. 75mm Mk. V gun)

The A.E.C. Mk. III was developed from an original private venture initiated by the Chief Engineer of Associated Equipment Co. Ltd. The Mk. I mounted a 2-pdr in a typical Valentine turret, but Marks II and III adopted a 75mm gun as main armament in a new turret, as seen here. The Mk. I reached a production of 122, and the remaining 507 were of the Mk. II and Mk. III model, for a total of 629 vehicles in all. They saw service mainly in the heavy troops of armored car squadrons.

1:35 scale

FEET

0   5   10   15   20

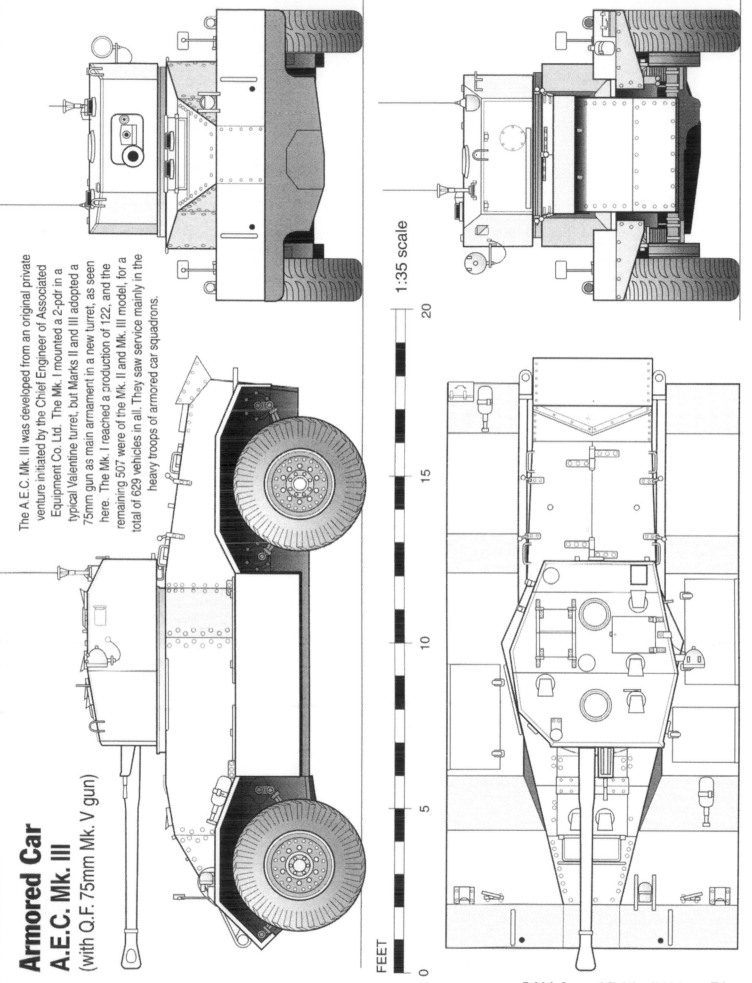

Armored Car, Humber, Mk. II

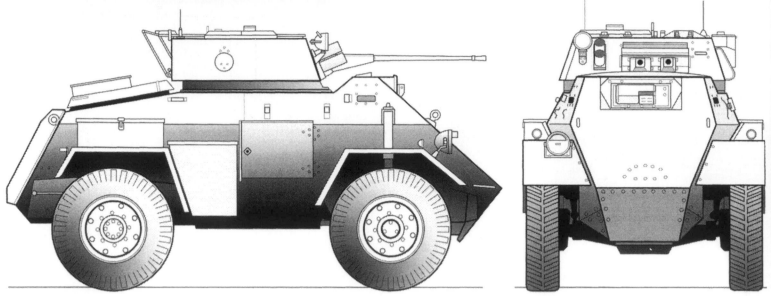

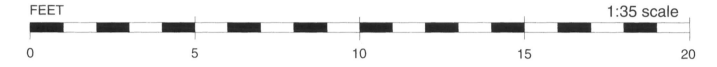

FEET

1:35 scale

0   5   10   15   20

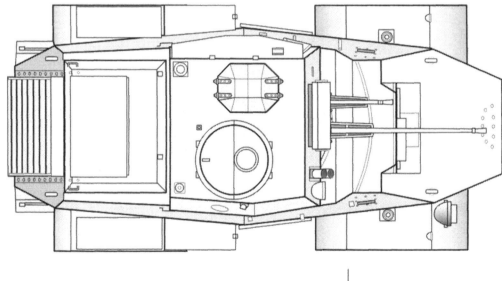

The hull of the Humber Mk. I was quickly deemed to be far too complex for production schedules, and after 300 vehicles, a new welded hull replaced the early riveted one. This hull would persist through Marks III and IV as well. The Mk. II's turret was basically identical to the Mk. I. The vehicle weight increased to 7.1 tons vs. 6.85, but the Mk. II showed no loss of speed or range (45mph/250 mi.). It was armed with 2 Besas, a Bren and two 4" smoke bomb throwers.

A grand total of 450 Mk. IIs were built and first began service in Egypt in early 1942.

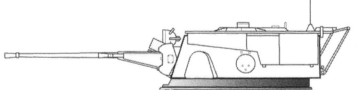

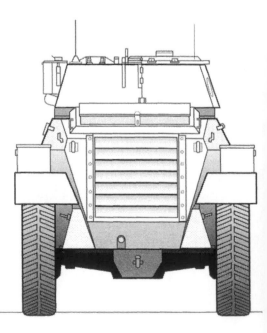

The first operational Humber Mk. IIs arrived in Egypt in early 1942, and had largely replaced the Mk. Is by the fall of that year. They had roomier interiors and heavier armor plate and were well accepted. As always the desert regiments altered the stowage arrangements to better suit their purposes. Sun compasses were welded to the right side of the turret, and many cars had extra stowage bins bolted to the lids of their hull side lockers. Racks for 4-gallon petrol and water cans were welded to the front mudguards, below the escape doors, and on the rear of the hull. They also carried a spare wheel on the glacis plate.

The majority of the 450 Mk. IIs built were sent to North Africa and the Middle East, and they were rarely seen elsewhere. They were used very successfully for long-range reconnaissance.

Car, 4x4 Reconnaissance
Morris Mk. II

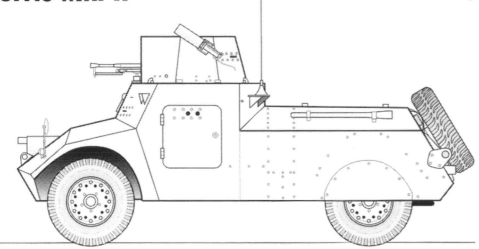

Side view with hatches raised and
Boys anti-tank rifle in firing position.

The Morris Mk. I was a rear engined, 4x2
rear wheel drive vehicle with a smooth
enclosed underbelly that gave it quite good
cross-country capability. The driver was in
the center at front, and the gunner in a
turret to his right, and a third man operating
a Boys to his right.

On the 4x4 wheeled Mk. II version, the
coil springs were replaced with leaf springs.
Approximately 2,200 Morris Light Reconnaissance Cars, both Mk. I and Mk. II, were
built, including turretless OP versions.

Spare tire not
shown on top
view for sake
of clarity.

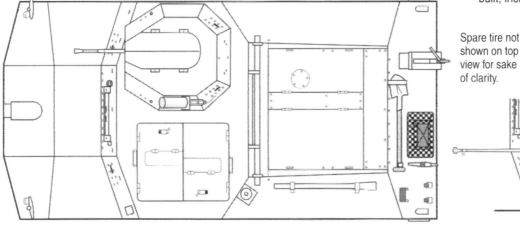

Top view of hatches up and Boys
anti-tank rifle in firing position.

FEET

0   5   10   15   20

1:35 scale

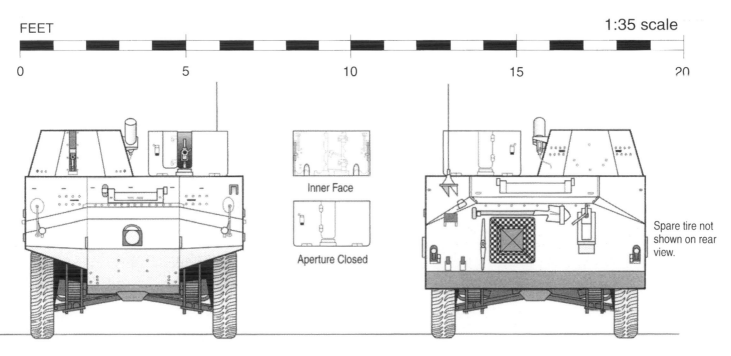

Inner Face

Aperture Closed

Spare tire not
shown on rear
view.

Churchill NA75
with 75mm Sherman gun

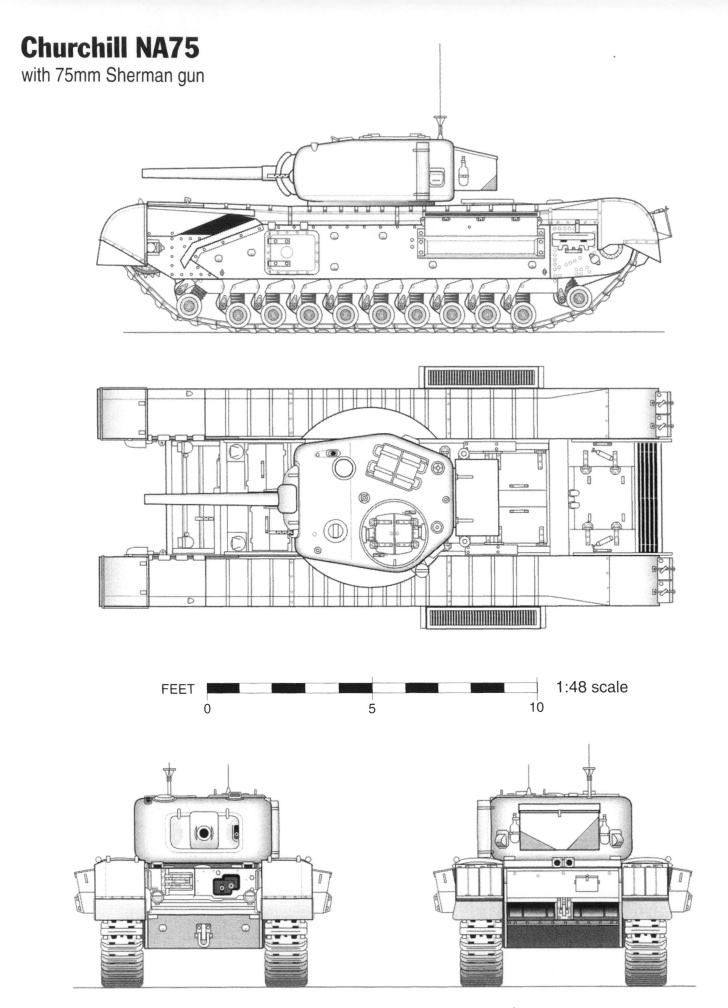

FEET

0   5   10

1:48 scale

Light Tank Mk. VII
"Tetrarch"
Fitted with Littlejohn adaptor

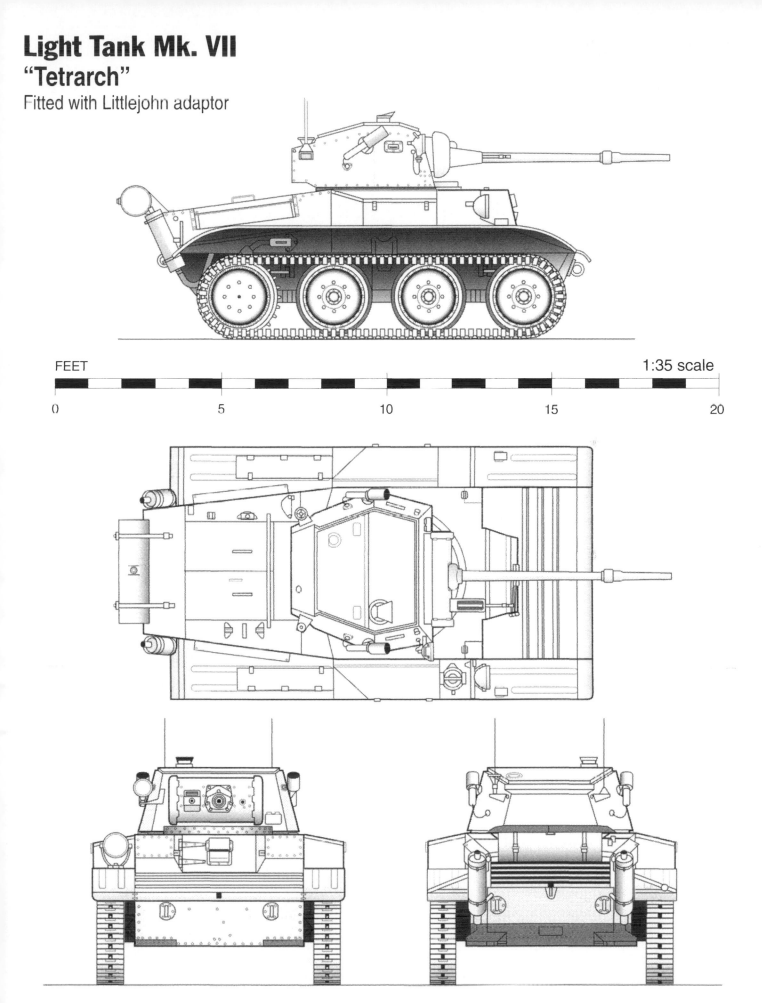

FEET

1:35 scale

0   5   10   15   20

Stuart V, M3A3 Recce
in British, Canadian and Polish service

Various models of the Stuart light tank were sent to support British and Commonwealth countries early in the war. Conversion of these tanks for use in the reconnainssance and gun-towing role began with the redundant Stuart I in Tunisia, and persisted right up to the Stuart V in Europe and Italy.

In Burma they are shown with a rounded screen dome to protect them from hand grenades, etc. However, most had low metal plate rim welded around the turret opening to support machine gun mounts, and various light armament was mounted. A very elaborate folding canvas weather covering was tested, but was rarely seen in use in the field. However, an open-topped vehicle like this would most certainly require some sort of makeshift canvas cover for protection against heavy downpours and snow, and a rolled canvas can often be seen carried on the deck. A command version carried extra radio equipment for use by the unit commander.

It was normally used by armored regiments and armored reconnaissance regiments to feel out enemy positions on a regimental front.

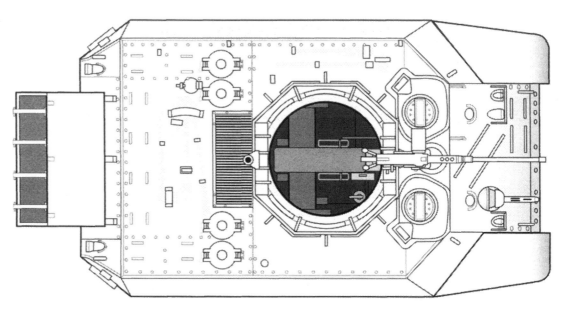

1:35 scale

FEET

0   5   10   15   20

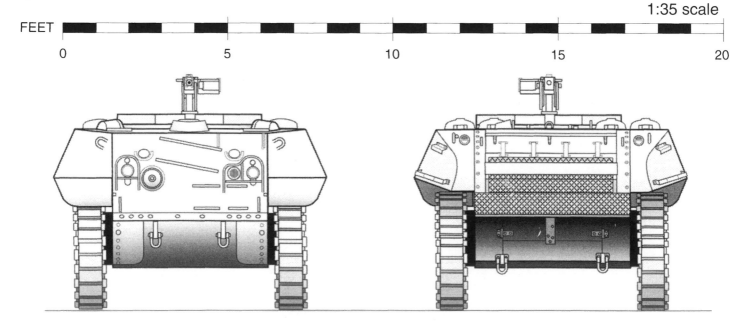

Sherman VC
"Firefly"

17-pounder armed M4A4 in
British, Commonwealth and Polish service

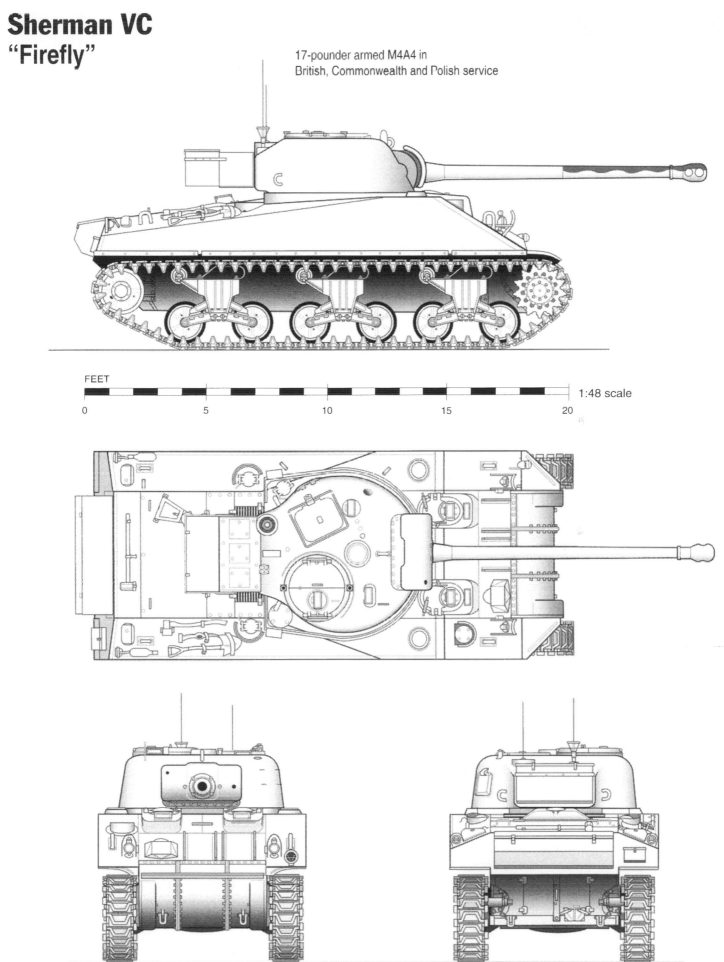

FEET

0   5   10   15   20

1:48 scale

Sherman IC Hybrid
"Firefly"

17-pounder armed M4 Hybrid in
British and Canadian service.

Old can or heavy wrapping where cammo starts.
Chicken wire and foliage also used over the cammo.

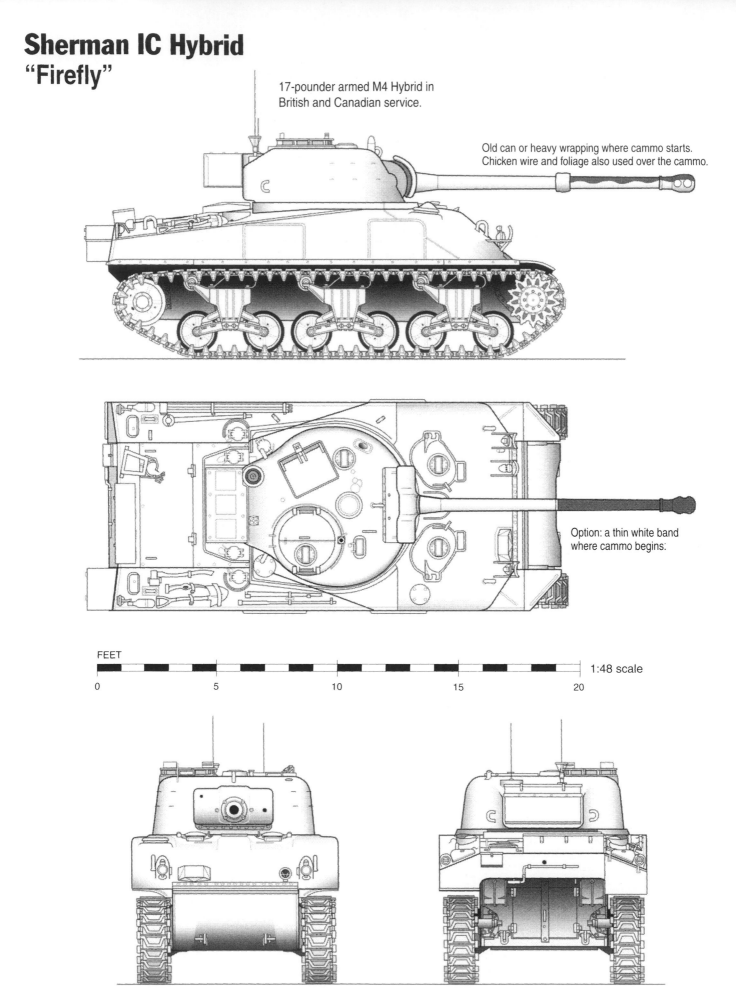

Option: a thin white band
where cammo begins:

FEET

0   5   10   15   20

1:48 scale

Infantry Tank Mk. IV (A22)
Churchill Mk. V
95mm Tank Howitzer

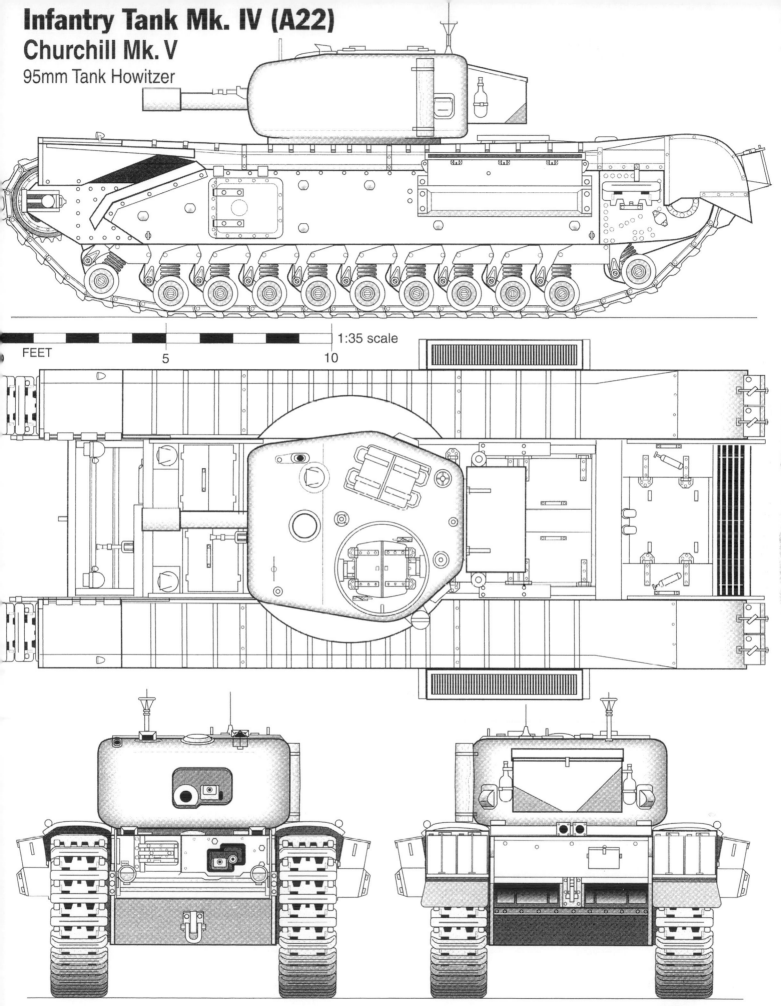

1:35 scale

FEET

5   10

M3 CDL (Canal Defense Light)

On early M3 medium fitted with 75mm gun M2.

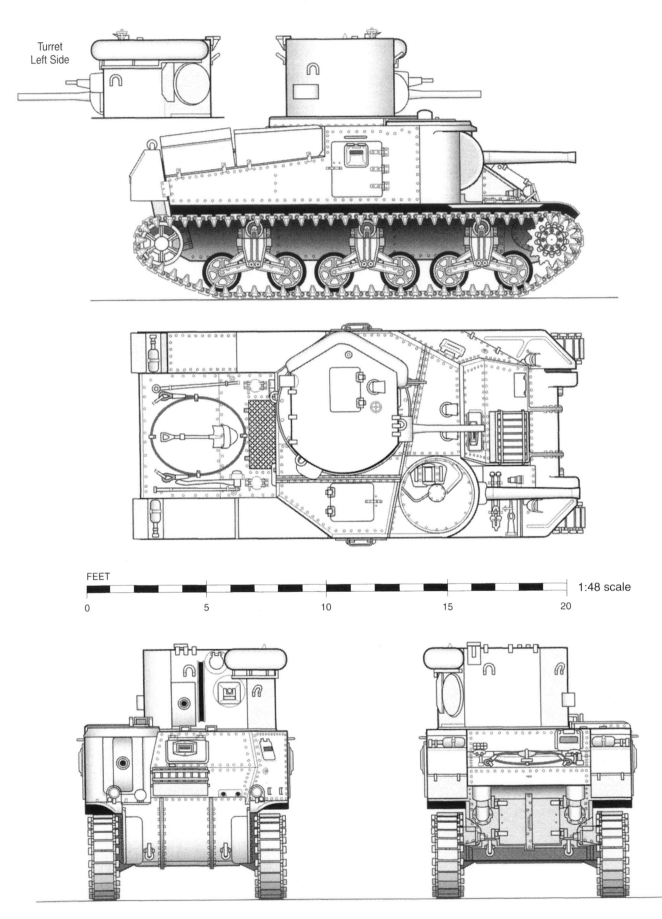

Turret
Left Side

FEET

0   5   10   15   20

1:48 scale

Two views of the Valentine Mk. XI mounting a 75mm main gun.

Infantry Tank
Valentine Mk. XI

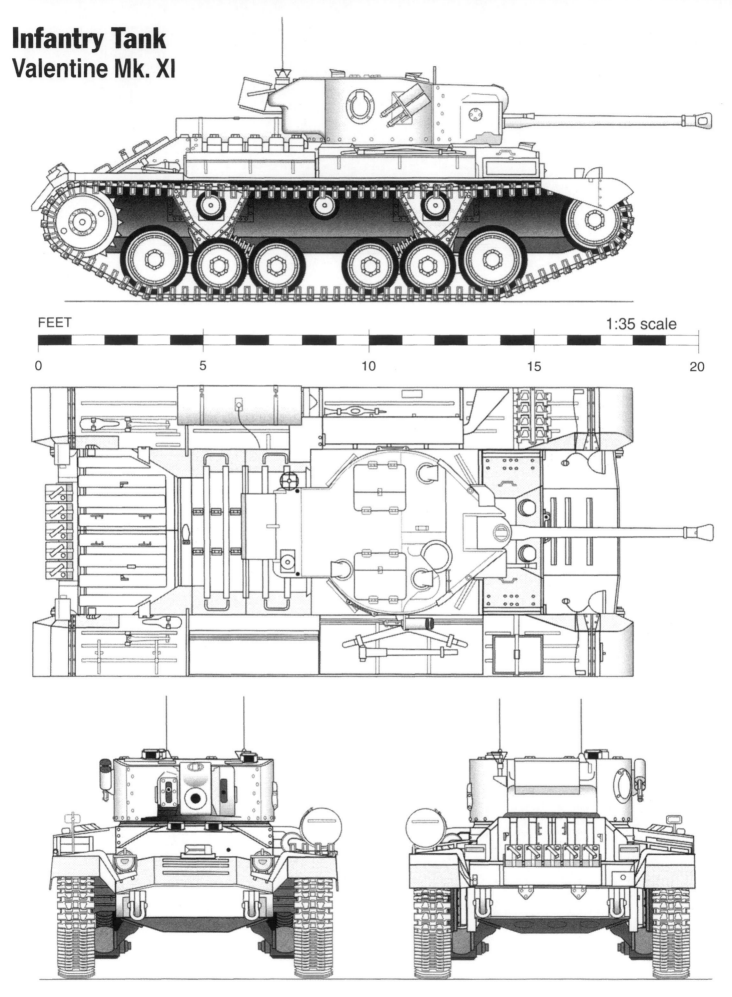

FEET

1:35 scale

0   5   10   15   20

Cruiser Tank, Comet (A34)
(mounting the 77mm shortened 17-pdr gun)

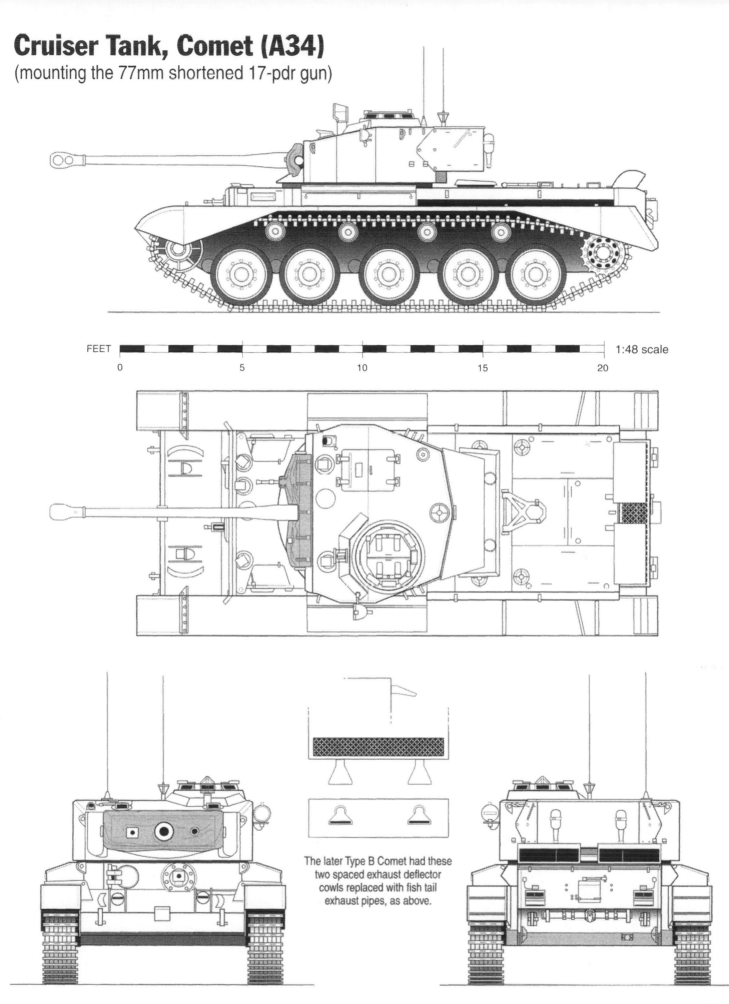

FEET 0   5   10   15   20   1:48 scale

The later Type B Comet had these two spaced exhaust deflector cowls replaced with fish tail exhaust pipes, as above.

Excellent front (top) and rear (bottom) views of the Comet cruiser tank.

Churchill 3" Gun Carrier
Mk. I (A22D)

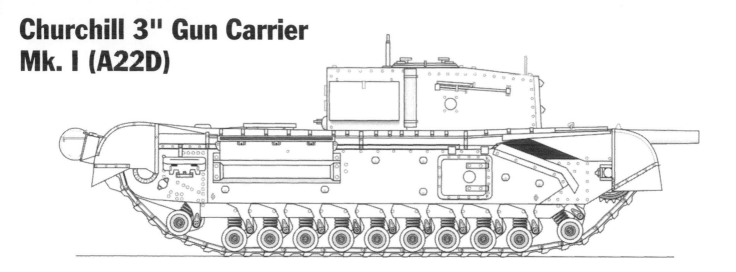

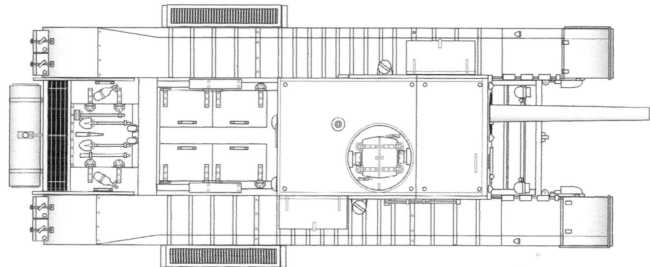

FEET   1:48 scale

0   5   10   15   20

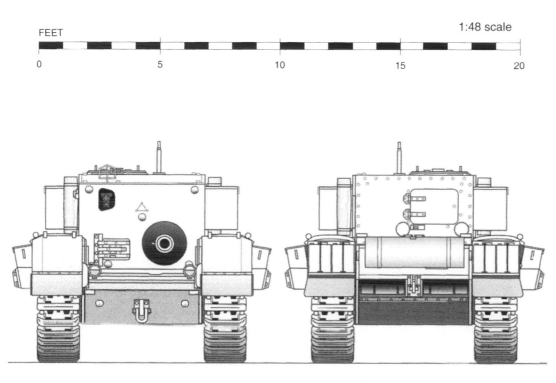

In 1941 a desperate attempt was made to field a gun powerful enough to defeat German armor in the event of an invasion. The design simply had to be quick and effective, using the heaviest anti-tank weapon available. The 3" AA gun of 1914 vintage was gradually being replaced by the superb new 3.7" weapon, thus freeing up these 3" guns for this anti-tank project.

The A22 Churchill was chosen as the logical chassis choice and on 25 July 1941 a contract for 100 "Tanks A22 Special Type (Churchill 3 inch 20 cwt Self Propelled Mounting)" was placed with Vauxhall Motors. However, this was later changed to 24 machines, and in January 1942 was again increased to 50. Eventually all 50 were completed by November 1942 and given the official nomenclature of "Carrier, Churchill 3 in. Gun Mk. I". Frontal armor was 89mm while side plates were 76mm. It carried a crew of four.

Eventually, all plans for using these S/P guns in combat were dropped and all but one of them were eventually converted to armored recovery vehicles.

Avenger (A30)

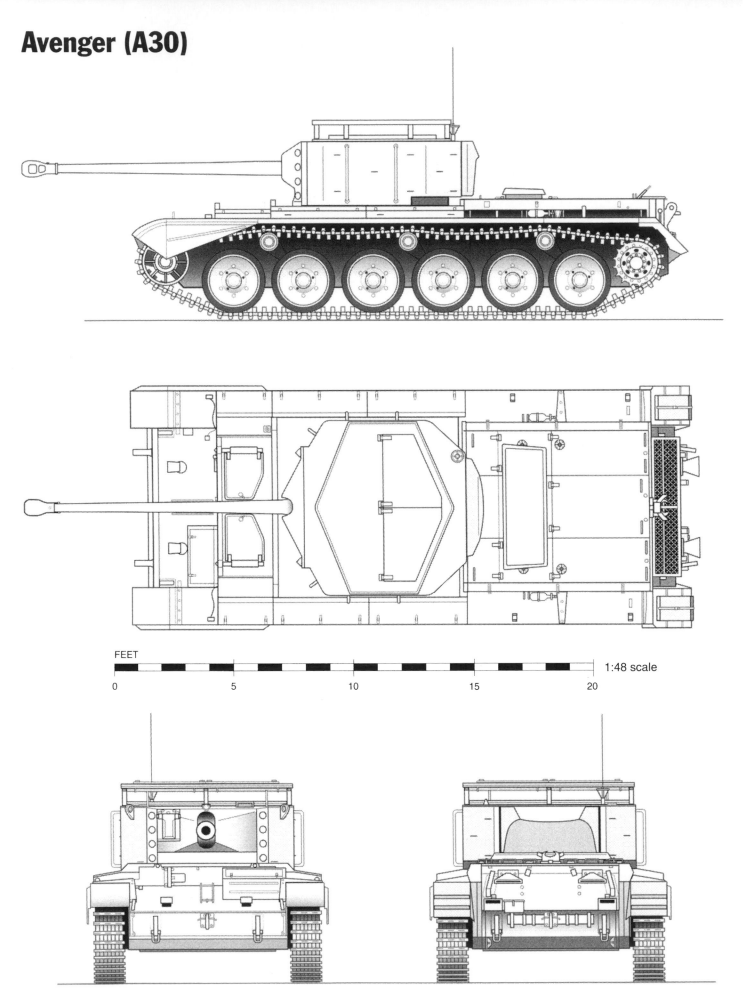

FEET

0   5   10   15   20   1:48 scale

The Avenger was developed a bit too late for service in World War II, but it shows the direction that planners were going in order to mount the deadly 17-pounder on as many chassis as possible to take on German armor. In essence, the Avenger was an artillery weapon, but it was based on the Challenger chassis.

Infantry Tank
Black Prince
(A43)

Intended as an improved version of the Churchill with a 17-pounder gun, this project was begun near the end of 1943, and six test vehicles had been completed by the time the war ended in early 1945.

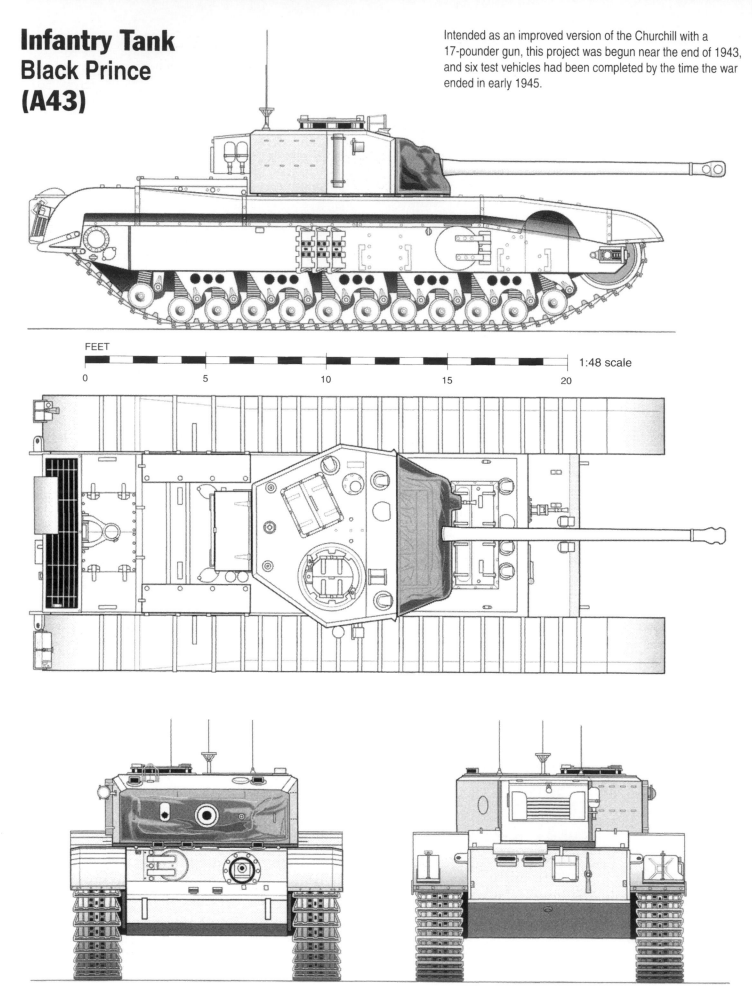

FEET

0   5   10   15   20

1:48 scale

A39 "Tortoise" Assault Tank

Mounting a 32-pdr gun, this project was begun in 1943 and six prototypes were finished by 1947.

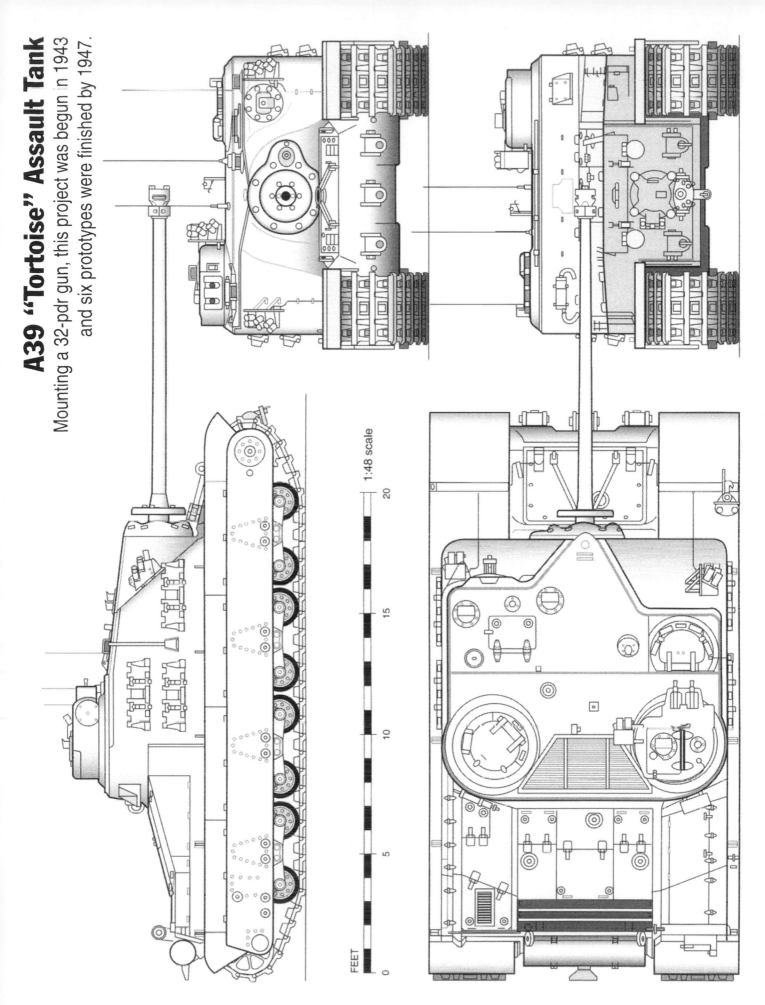

1:48 scale

FEET

0   5   10   15   20

Centurion Mk. I
A41 prototype, pilot no. 2

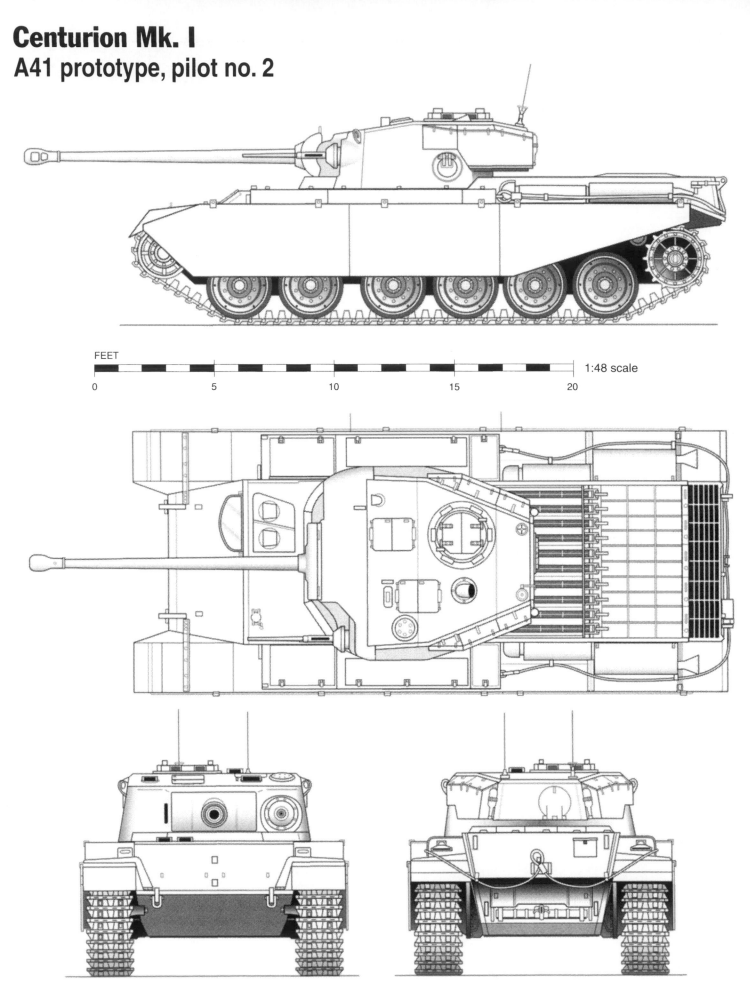

FEET

0   5   10   15   20

1:48 scale

BIBLIOGRAPHY

Chamberlain, P., and C. Ellis. *British and American Tanks of World War II*. London: Arms and Armour Press, 1969.

———. *The Churchill Tank*. London: Arms and Armour Press, 1971.

———. *Making Tracks: British Carrier Story*. Windsor, England: Profile Publications Ltd., 1973.

———. *The Sherman: An Illustrated History of the M4 Medium Tank*. London: Arms and Armour Press, 1968.

———. *Tanks of the World, 1915–45*. London: Arms and Armour Press, 1972.

Fletcher, D. *Crusader and Covenanter Cruiser Tanks, 1939–45*. London: Osprey Publishing, 2005.

———. *Mr. Churchill's Tank: The British Infantry Tank Mark IV*. Atglen, PA: Schiffer Pubishing Ltd., 1999.

———. *Tanks in Camera, 1940–1943*. Stroud, England: Sutton Publishing Ltd., 1998.

Forty, G. *A Photo History of Armoured Cars in Two World Wars*. Poole, England: Blandford Press, 1984.

———. *United States Tanks of World War II*. Poole, England: Blandford Press, 1983.

Foss, C. F. *The Encyclopedia of Tanks and Armoured Fighting Vehicles*. London: Amber Books Ltd., 2002.

Hayward, M. *Sherman Firefly*. Tiptree, England: Barbarossa Books, 2001.

Henry, H. G. *Dieppe through the Lens, after the Battle*. London: Plaistow Press Limited, 1994.

Hunnicutt, R. P. *Armored Car: A History of American Wheeled Combat Vehicles*. Novato, CA: Presidio Press, 2002.

———. *Sherman: A History of the American Medium Tank*. Bellmont, CA: Raurus Enterprises, 1978.

Icks, Robert J. *Encyclopedia of Armoured Cars* Secaucus, NJ: Chartwell Books, Inc., Secaucus, 1976.

———. *Encyclopedia of Tanks*. London: Barrie & Jenkins Ltd., 1975.

———. *Tanks and Armored Vehicles, 1900–1945*. Old Greenwich, CT: We Inc., 1967.

Jentz, T. L. *Tank Combat in North Africa*. Atglen, PA: Schiffer Publishing Ltd., 1998.

Perrett, B. *The Valentine in North Africa, 1942–43*. Shepperton, England: Ian Allan Ltd., 1972.

The Tank Museum. *Churchill Tank: Vehicle History and Specifications*. London: Her Majesty's Stationery Office, 1983.

White, B. T. *British Armoured Cars, 1914–1945*. Hampton Court, England: Ian Allan Ltd.

———. *British Tank Markings and Names*. London: Arms and Armour Press, 1978.

———. *British Tanks and Fighting Vehicles, 1914–1945*. Shepperton, England: Ian Allan Ltd., 1970.

———. *British Tanks, 1915–1945*. Hampton Court, England: Ian Allan Ltd.

Basic Tank Components

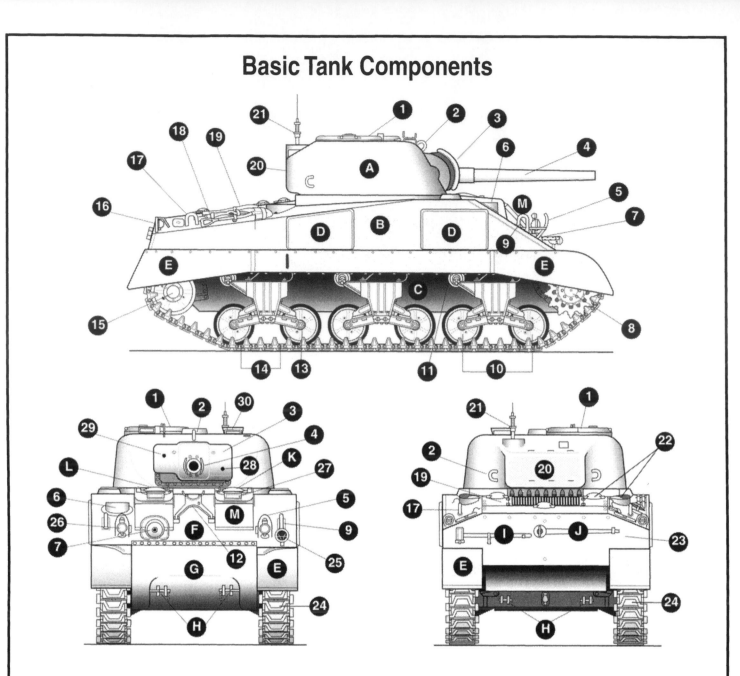

A. Cast Turret
B. Upper Hull
C. Lower Hull
D. Appliqué Armor
E. Dust Skirt
F. Glacis Plate
G. Transmission Housing
H. Towing Brackets
 I. Sledge Hammer
J. Idler Adjusting Wrench
K. Driver's Hatch
L. Assist. Driver Hatch
M. Angled 1" Plate

1. Commander's Hatch
2. Turret Lift Hook
3. Gun Mantlet
4. Main Gun
5. Headlamp Guard
6. Ventilator
7. Bow Machinegun
8. Drive Sprocket
9. Hull Lift Hook
10. Bogie Suspension Unit
11. Trailing Return Roller
12. Gun Lock
13. Road Wheel
14. Track Links
15. Rear Idler Wheel
16. Tail Lights

17. Chassis Lift Hook
18. Tools
19. Engine Deck
20. Turret Bustle
21. Radio Aerial
22. Fuel Filler Caps
23. Rear Plate
24. Track Shoe
25. Siren
26. Driving Light
27. Driver's Periscope
28. Coaxial Machine Gun
29. Main Gun Sight
30. Loader's Periscope

VARIOUS MODELING SCALES

Scale	1 inch equals	1 scale foot =	1 scale meter =	Comments
1:4	4"	3"	250.0 mm	Flying Models, Live-steam Trains
1:8	8"	1 1/2"	125.0 mm	Cars, Motorcycles, Trains
1:12	1'	1"	83.3 mm	Cars, Motorcycles, Dollhouses
1:16	1' 4"	3/4"	62.5 mm	Cars, Motorcycles, Trains
1:20	1' 8"	19/32"	50.0 mm	Cars
1:22.5	1' 10 1/2"	17/32"	44.4 mm	G-Scale Trains
1:24	2'	1/2"	41.7 mm	Cars, Trucks, Dollhouses
1:25	2' 1"	15/32"	40.0 mm	Cars, Trucks
1:32	2' 8"	3/8"	31.25 mm	Aircraft, Cars, Tanks, Trains
1:35	2' 11"	11/32"	28.57 mm	Armor
1:43	3' 7"	9/32"	23.25 mm	Cars, Trucks
1:48	4'	1/4"	20.83 mm	Aircraft, Armor, O-Scale Trains
1:64	5' 4"	3/16"	15.62 mm	Aircraft, S-Scale Trains
1:72	6'	11/63"	13.88 mm	Aircraft, Armor, Boats
1:76	6' 4"	5/32"	13.16 mm	Armor
1:87	7' 3"	—	11.49 mm	Armor, HO-Scale Trains
1:96	8'	1/8"	10.42 mm	1/8" Scale Ships, Aircraft
1:100	8' 4"	—	10.00 mm	Aircraft
1:125	10' 5"	—	8.00 mm	Aircraft
1:144	12'	—	6.94 mm	Aircraft
1:160	13' 4"	—	6.25 mm	N-Scale Trains
1:192	16'	1/16"	5.21 mm	1/16" Scale Ships
1:200	16' 8"	—	5.00 mm	Aircraft, Ships

Stackpole Military History Series

THE AMERICAN CIVIL WAR

Cavalry Raids of the Civil War
Ghost, Thunderbolt, and Wizard
Pickett's Charge
Witness to Gettysburg

WORLD WAR II

Armor Battles of the Waffen-SS, 1943–45
Army of the West
Australian Commandos
The B-24 in China
Backwater War
The Battle of Sicily
Beyond the Beachhead
The Brandenburger Commandos
The Brigade
Bringing the Thunder
Coast Watching in World War II
Colossal Cracks
D-Day to Berlin
Dive Bomber!
Eagles of the Third Reich
Exit Rommel
Fist from the Sky
Flying American Combat Aircraft of
    World War II
Forging the Thunderbolt
Fortress France
The German Defeat in the East, 1944–45
German Order of Battle, Vol. 1
German Order of Battle, Vol. 2
German Order of Battle, Vol. 3
Germany's Panzer Arm in World War II
GI Ingenuity
Grenadiers
Infantry Aces
Iron Arm
Iron Knights
Kampfgruppe Peiper at the Battle
    of the Bulge

Luftwaffe Aces
Massacre at Tobruk
Messerschmitts over Sicily
Michael Wittmann, Vol. 1
Michael Wittmann, Vol. 2
Mountain Warriors
The Nazi Rocketeers
On the Canal
Packs On!
Panzer Aces
Panzer Aces II
The Panzer Legions
Panzers in Winter
The Path to Blitzkrieg
Retreat to the Reich
Rommel's Desert War
The Savage Sky
A Soldier in the Cockpit
Soviet Blitzkrieg
Stalin's Keys to Victory
Surviving Bataan and Beyond
T-34 in Action
Tigers in the Mud
The 12th SS, Vol. 1
The 12th SS, Vol. 2
The War against Rommel's Supply Lines

THE COLD WAR / VIETNAM

Flying American Combat Aircraft:
    The Cold War
Here There Are Tigers
Land with No Sun
Street without Joy

WARS OF THE MIDDLE EAST

Never-Ending Conflict

GENERAL MILITARY HISTORY

Carriers in Combat
Desert Battles

Real Battles. Real Soldiers. Real Stories.